All New Easy
TRUE STORIES

A PICTURE-BASED BEGINNING READER

by Sandra Heyer

Longman

In memory of Auntie Ann, teller of the famous nightgown story.
Yes, I remember you.

All New Easy True Stories

Copyright © 2004 by Pearson Education, Inc.
All rights reserved.

Pearson Education, 10 Bank Street, White Plains, NY 10606

Executive editor: Laura Ledrean
Development editor: John Barnes
Senior production editor: Robert Ruvo
Marketing manager: Joe Chapple
Director of manufacturing: Patrice Fraccio
Senior manufacturing buyer: Dave Dickey
Photo research: Dana Klinek
Cover design: Elizabeth Carlson
Text composition: ElectraGraphics, Inc.
Text font: 11/13 Palatino
Illustrations: Don Martinetti
Text credits and photo credits: see page 89

Library of Congress Cataloging-in-Publication Data

Heyer, Sandra.
     All new easy true stories / by Sandra Heyer.
          p.   cm.
     ISBN 0-13-118265-X (pbk. : alk. paper)
     1. English language—Textbooks for foreign speakers.   2. Readers.   I.
Title.
   PE1128.H43546   2004
   428.6'4—dc22

                                                        2003025452

ISBN: 0-13-118265-X

Printed in the United States of America
     6 7 8 9 10—BAH—08 07

Contents

Introduction iv

UNIT 1   **Give Me the Money!** 2

UNIT 2   **License, Please** 6

UNIT 3   **Mr. Venezuela** 10

UNIT 4   **Speed** 14

UNIT 5   **Grandfather Hada's Favorite Soup** 18

UNIT 6   **Handsome Again?** 22

UNIT 7   **A Super Soaker and a Super Kid** 26

UNIT 8   **The Flying Lesson** 30

UNIT 9   **Hawaiian Vacation** 34

UNIT 10   **Election Day** 38

UNIT 11   **The Best Doctor** 42

UNIT 12   **The Bottle** 46

UNIT 13   **Hold On, Joe** 50

UNIT 14   **Whose Money Is It?** 54

UNIT 15   **The Silver Porsche** 58

UNIT 16   **An Easy Job** 62

UNIT 17   **The Pet Rabbit** 66

UNIT 18   **The Birthday Present** 70

UNIT 19   **The Fire** 74

UNIT 20   **Nothing's Changed** 78

To the Teacher 83

Answer Key 90

Introduction

All New Easy True Stories is a low-beginning reader for students of English. It is a companion book to *Easy True Stories*; that is, it is written at the same reading level and has the same format. However, as the title indicates, it has all new stories and exercises.

PURPOSE

Why does the *True Stories* series offer two books at the low-beginning level? First, some students need more time at the low-beginning level before moving on to *True Stories in the News*, the next book in the series. This is particularly true for students with only basic literacy skills in their native languages. *All New Easy True Stories* gives students the option of lingering a while at this level. They can go back and forth between *Easy True Stories* and *All New Easy True Stories*, or they can complete first one book and then the other. (Students can read either book first.) Second, many teachers like to incorporate reading into their thematically-based instructional units; for example, "The Best Doctor" (*All New Easy True Stories*) adds dimension to any healthcare unit. With forty low-level stories, teachers have multiple opportunities to match readings with other classroom activities. Third, a choice of two books helps veteran teachers keep their lessons fresh: They can use *Easy True Stories* one semester and *All New Easy True Stories* the next. Alternating between the two books also keeps the lessons fresh for students who choose to stay in a low-beginning class when their classmates move on to the next level. They can essentially repeat the class but with all new material.

Easy True Stories and *All New Easy True Stories* can also be used in higher-level classes as the basis of a cooperative reading/speaking/listening activity. One group of students reads a story in one book while another group reads a story in the other book. Then, in pairs, students from one group tell their story to students from the other group, using the nine drawings as cues as they retell the story.

DESCRIPTION

All New Easy True Stories contains 20 units, each centered on a story that was adapted from a newspaper or magazine article. In answer to those students who think that some stories are too amazing to be true: Yes, the stories are true, to the best of our knowledge. The bear really did cure the woman of her knee problem, and the boy really did keep two puppies alive with his squirt gun. In the back of the book, you will find a special To the Teacher section with more information about each story.

HOW TO USE ALL NEW EASY TRUE STORIES

Each unit is divided into three sections: Pre-reading, Reading, and Post-reading Exercises. Following are some suggestions for using each of the sections. Teachers new to the field might find these suggestions especially helpful. Please keep in mind that these are only suggestions. Teachers should, of course, feel free to adapt these strategies to best suit their teaching styles and their students' learning styles.

PRE-READING

Read the story aloud to students as they look at the drawings on the Pre-reading page. Begin by saying "Number One" and slowly reading the sentences that the first picture illustrates. Then say "Number Two" and read the appropriate sentences. Continue in this manner. Saying the numbers of the pictures while telling the story ensures that all eyes are on the same picture.

Sometimes in reading the story aloud, you might want to break it down into even smaller chunks of meaning. In Unit 17, for example, the story begins, "Mrs. Nunn is at the supermarket with her three children." Instead of reading this exactly as it is written, you might say, "Her name is Mrs. Nunn. She is a mother. She has three children. She is at the supermarket with her children." Breaking the story down into smaller pieces of information and pausing between the pieces gives students more time to digest the information.

You may wish to invite students to actively participate as you tell the story. Again, Unit 17 provides an example. Holding up your book, point to the drawing of the woman in frame 1 and say, "It's a man." Then pause and wait for students to correct the statement. If they are silent, repeat the statement, this time with rising intonation: "It's a man?" When students say, "No, it's a woman," confirm that they are correct by nodding and repeating, "It's a woman." Point to the drawing again and say, "She's a father." When students say, "No, she's a mother," nod and repeat, "She's a mother." Continue with obviously false statements ("She has five children." "She's at the gas station.") and let students correct them. This back-and-forth activity keeps the class engaged as you tell the story. It also reassures them that although there are new words in the story, there are also many familiar words.

If you have access to an overhead projector, you could make transparencies of the pre-reading pages and show them this way, rather than having students follow in their textbooks. Then it is easier to point to the drawings as you tell the story. With erasable markers, you can draw arrows to items, add drawings of your own, or write words next to the pictures.

You will probably want to walk away from the pictures from time to time and act out some scenes, perhaps with the help of props. Alternately, you can dispense with the pre-reading drawings entirely and act out the whole story, writing key words on the board during your "performance." Stories with plenty of action, like "An Easy Job," lend themselves to this dramatic introduction.

After telling the story, you might want to check comprehension by reciting lines from the story and asking students to say the numbers of the corresponding pictures. Or, to bring students one step closer to reading, you could write key words on the board and ask students to say the numbers of the drawings in which those words are depicted. (To keep the atmosphere relaxed, call on the whole group for the answers, rather than on individuals.)

Some of the stories build suspense. You might stop short of the last few sentences when reading those stories aloud and ask students to guess how the story ends.

READING

After listening to the story, students read the story silently, or you read the story aloud. To keep the students engaged, you can make "mistakes" as you read. For example, you could read the story in Unit 1 this way: "Late one night, a man walks into a store. It is a big store. It has ten cash registers and ten cashiers." Pause after each sentence, letting students speak in chorus to correct the mistake, rather than calling on individuals. Young students in particular respond enthusiastically to this technique.

In a beginning class there is often a wide range of reading proficiency. Some students understand every word they read, while others get only the gist of the story. Assure students in the latter category that it is not essential to understand every word. The ability to be comfortable with a certain amount of ambiguity is a great asset to a beginning reader.

POST-READING EXERCISES

Vocabulary and Comprehension   Students can complete the exercises individually, in pairs, in small groups, or with the whole class. The exercises can be completed in class or assigned as homework.

Discussion   The discussion exercises require students to complete a task—to fill in a chart, to answer questions, to draw a picture—so that there is a concrete focus to the activity. Several of the discussion exercises ask students to respond to statements by circling *YES* or *NO*. Some of the statements, such as "I think beauty contests for women are a good idea," invite further comments. Some students will expand on their answers; others will simply answer the question. It is best not to make a big fuss over students' reticence. Beginning students need a "silent period" before they begin to speak, during which they try to make sense of the new language. Students who do not talk much may simply need a longer silent period than their more talkative classmates. Others are simply uncomfortable sharing personal opinions in a large group.

Writing   Most of the writing exercises are designed to produce error-free writing; students simply rework the information in the discussion exercise. Other writing exercises will result in writing that is not free from errors. Some teachers may choose to correct the errors, while others may not; here teachers must use their own judgment.

The vocabulary, comprehension, discussion, and writing exercises are at approximately parallel levels; that is, they assume that students speak and write about as well as they read. Of course, that is not always the case. Students in a beginning class can have a wide range of experience with English, as you may know only too well. Some students are at the beginning level in all the skills areas—reading, writing, speaking, and listening. Other students may have well-developed speaking and listening skills, but low-level literacy skills. Another group may have studied English in their native countries, perhaps for years, and are fairly proficient readers and writers, but were placed in a beginning class because they are unable to speak or understand spoken English. So, you may have to tailor the exercises—to adjust them up or down, to skip some, or to add some of your own.

Both the exercises and reading selections are intended to build students' confidence along with their reading skills. Above all, it is hoped that reading *All New Easy True Stories* will be a pleasure, for both you and your students.

UNIT 1

1. PRE-READING

Look at the pictures. Listen to your teacher tell the story.

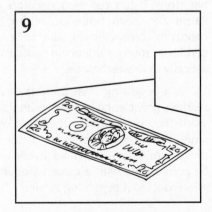

Give Me the Money!

EARLY one morning, a man walks into a store. It is a small store. It has only one cash register and one cashier.

The man has a $20 bill in his hand. He puts the money on the counter. "Do you have change for a twenty?" the man asks the cashier. "I don't think so," the cashier says. "But I'll look." The cashier opens the cash register.

The man shows the cashier a gun. Then he shows the cashier a bag. "Give me all the money!" the man says. "Put it in the bag!"

"But . . . " the cashier says.

"Give me all the money!" the man says. "Put it in the bag!"

"But . . . " the cashier says.

"Give me all the money!" the man shouts. "Put it in the bag!"

The cashier puts all the money in the bag. The man takes the bag and runs out of the store.

Later the man opens the bag. What is in it? All the money from the cash register— 15 dollars.

What is on the counter at the small store? The man's $20 bill.

2. VOCABULARY

Match the words and the pictures. Write your answer on the line.

cash register   bag   counter
gun $20 bill   cashier

1. ___cash register___   2. _____   3. _____

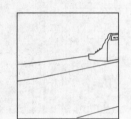

4. _____   5. _____   6. _____

3. COMPREHENSION

REMEMBERING DETAILS

Which sentence is correct? Circle *a* or *b*.

1. **a.** Late one night, a man walks into a store.
    b. Early one morning, a man walks into a store.

2. **a.** It is a small store.
    b. It is a big store.

3. **a.** He asks the cashier, "Do you have change for a ten?"
    b. He asks the cashier, "Do you have change for a twenty?"

4. **a.** "Give me all the money," the man says quietly.
    b. "Give me all the money!" the man shouts.

5. **a.** The man takes the bag and runs out of the store.
    b. The man takes the bag and walks out of the store.

REVIEWING THE STORY

Write the correct word on the line.

A man walks into a small store. "Do you have _____*change*_____ for a
$20 bill?" he asks the cashier. When the cashier _____2_____ the cash
register, the man _____3_____ him a gun and a bag. "Give me all the
_____4_____!" the man shouts.

The cashier gives the man _____5_____ the money from the cash
register—$15. The man runs away with the money. He leaves his $20 bill on the counter
at the small _____6_____.

4. DISCUSSION

A. In the story, the cashier opens the cash register in a small store. There is $15 in the
cash register. In the United States, how much money is usually in the cash register at
a small store?

In a small group, take a guess. Write your group's answer here: $_____

B. Imagine this: A man walks into a small store in the United States and shows the
cashier a gun. "Give me all the money!" the man says. The cashier gives the man all
the money, and the man runs away. Later, the police catch the man. How long is the
man in prison?

In a small group, take a guess. Write your group's answer here: _____ years

Tell the class your group's answers. (The correct answers are on page 82.)

5. WRITING

A. **Prepare for a dictation. Practice with the sentences below. Follow the directions on
page 82.**

1. Walk into the store.
2. Put money on the counter.
3. Show the cashier a gun.
4. Run out of the store.
5. Open the bag.

B. **Now close your book. On your own paper, write the sentences as your teacher says
them. Then open your book and check your writing.**

1. PRE-READING

Look at the pictures. Listen to your teacher tell the story.

License, Please

A MAN is driving a big black car through the mountains in Norway. He is driving fast.

A police officer sees the black car and follows it.

The black car goes around a curve. Then it goes around another curve. How fast is the black car going? It is going ten kilometers over the speed limit. That is too fast for the curves.

The police officer turns on his red light and his siren. The black car slows down, pulls over to the side of the road, and stops. The police car pulls over and stops, too.

The police officer walks to the black car. "License, please," he says. The man in the black car shows the police officer his license.

"Oh!" the police officer says and smiles. "Well! Have a nice day, sir," he says. Then he walks back to his police car and drives away.

The police officer doesn't give the man a ticket. Why not? The man in the black car was driving too fast, wasn't he? Yes, he was. But he is the king of Norway.

2. VOCABULARY

Match the words and the pictures. Write your answer on the line.

pull over   curve   license
mountains   king   follow

1. _____*mountains*_____   2. _____   3. _____

4. _____   5. _____   6. _____

3. COMPREHENSION

REMEMBERING DETAILS

Complete the sentences. Write your answer on the line.

1. The man is driving a big white car, right?

   No, he is driving a big _____**black car**_____.

2. The man is driving through the mountains in Peru, right?

   No, he is driving through the mountains in _____.

3. He is driving slowly, right?

   No, he is driving _____.

4. The car is going five kilometers over the speed limit, right?

   No, it is going _____.

5. The man is the president of Norway, right?

   No, he is the _____.

MAKING CONNECTIONS

Complete the sentences. Write the letter of your answer on the line.

1. The police officer sees the black car and ___d___

2. The black car pulls over and _____

3. The police officer walks to the black car and _____

4. The police officer looks at the man's license and _____

5. The police officer walks back to his car and _____

a. smiles.

b. drives away.

c. says, "License, please."

d. follows it.

e. stops.

4. DISCUSSION

These people are driving too fast. Do they get a ticket in your country? Tell the class.

1. the president of your country

2. the president's brother

3. a tourist from another country

4. a rich man
(He is holding money in his hand.)

5. WRITING

Make four sentences with the information in the discussion exercise. For example:

The president of my country doesn't get a ticket.

The president's brother gets a ticket.

Now write your sentences on your own paper.

1. PRE-READING

Look at the pictures. Listen to your teacher tell the story.

Mr. Venezuela

EVERY year, there is a beauty contest in Venezuela. The most beautiful woman is the winner. She is "Miss Venezuela."

Now there is another beauty contest in Venezuela. It is for men only. The most handsome man is the winner. He is "Mr. Venezuela."

Johnny Alvarez, age 23, wants to be Mr. Venezuela, so he is working hard. He is lifting weights, and he is running. He is eating a special diet, too. He is eating only fruit, vegetables, and chicken. He is not eating bread, ice cream, or candy. He wants to look good for the contest.

Why does Johnny want to be Mr. Venezuela? He is a model. "If I am Mr. Venezuela," he says, "I will get a lot of modeling work."

Some men don't like the Mr. Venezuela contest. "Beauty contests are for women," they say. "They are not for men."

But women like the Mr. Venezuela contest. "We like to look at the men," the women say. "The men in Venezuela are the most handsome men in the world."

2. VOCABULARY

Match the words and the pictures. Write your answer on the line.

winner   beauty contest   lift weights
model   Venezuela

1. _beauty contest_

2. _winner_

3. _Venezuela_

4. _lift weights_

5. _model_

3. COMPREHENSION

REMEMBERING DETAILS

One word in each sentence is not correct. Find the word and cross it out. Write the correct word.

1. Every ~~month~~ *year*, there is a beauty contest in Venezuela.

2. The most intelligent woman is the winner.

3. Now there is another beauty contest for children only.

4. Johnny Alvarez is a doctor.

5. He is eating only fruit, vegetables, and pizza.

6. He is not eating bread, ice cream, or meat.

MAKING CONNECTIONS

Complete the sentences. Write the letter of your answer on the line.

1. Johnny Alvarez is lifting weights and running __b__

2. Johnny wants to be Mr. Venezuela __c__

3. Some men don't like the Mr. Venezuela contest __a__

4. Women like the Mr. Venezuela contest __d__

BECAUSE

a. they think beauty contests are not for men.

b. he wants to look good for the contest.

c. he wants to get modeling work.

d. they like to look at the handsome men.

4. DISCUSSION

Read the sentences. Circle *yes* or *no*. Then share your answers with the class.

1. In my country, there are beauty contests for women.   YES   NO
2. In my country, there are beauty contests for men.   YES   NO
3. I think beauty contests for women are a good idea.   YES   NO
4. I think beauty contests for men are a good idea.   YES   NO
5. I like to watch beauty contests.   YES   NO

5. WRITING

A. Imagine this: There is a beauty contest for women on TV. The most beautiful woman is the winner. Will you watch it? Write your answer on your own paper. For example:

Yes, I will watch it because . . .   OR   No, I won't watch it because . . .

B. Imagine this: There is a beauty contest for men on TV. The most handsome man is the winner. Will you watch it? Write your answer on your own paper.

UNIT 4

1. PRE-READING

Look at the pictures. Listen to your teacher tell the story.

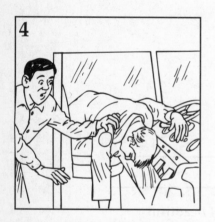

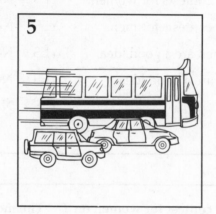

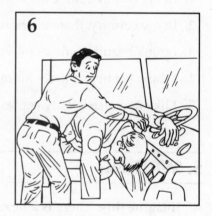

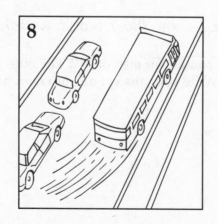

Speed

RAMYA is a waiter. He works at a restaurant from eight o'clock in the morning to four o'clock in the afternoon.

One day at four o'clock Ramya leaves work and gets on a bus to go home. He sits down behind the bus driver.

Suddenly the bus driver leans forward. His head is almost to the floor. Ramya jumps up. "Are you OK, sir?" he asks the bus driver. The bus driver doesn't answer.

The bus is going fast now, and nobody is driving it. Ramya pulls on the bus driver. He tries to pull him out of the driver's seat. But the bus driver is a big man. Ramya can't move him.

Now the bus is going really fast. Ramya has to stop the bus! He puts his hands on the steering wheel. He puts his left foot on the brake. He drives the bus to the right side of the street. Slowly, he stops the bus.

An ambulance arrives and takes the bus driver to the hospital. All the passengers on the bus are OK.

Ramya works at a restaurant. He is a waiter. But one day, for ten minutes, Ramya was a bus driver—a bus driver and a hero.

2. VOCABULARY

Write the correct word on the line.

passengers   steering wheel   brake
waiter   hero   behind

1. Ramya works at a restaurant. He brings people their food. He is a _____ *waiter* _____.

2. Ramya doesn't like to sit in the back of the bus. He likes to sit in the front of the bus, in the seat ___ behind ___ the bus driver.

3. Ramya wants to drive the bus to the side of the street, so he puts his hands on the ___ steering wheel ___

4. Ramya wants to stop the bus, so he puts his foot on the ___ brake ___.

5. How are the people on the bus? The ___ passengers ___ are all OK.

6. Ramya is not a bus driver, and he is not a big man, but he drives the bus and stops it. The passengers say, "Thank you, Ramya! Thank you!" Ramya is a ___ hero ___.

3. COMPREHENSION

REMEMBERING DETAILS

Which sentence is correct? Circle *a* or *b*.

1. a. Ramya gets on a train to go home.
   b. Ramya gets on a bus to go home. ⟵ circled

2. a. The bus driver leans backward.
   b. The bus driver leans forward. ⟵ circled

3. a. The bus driver's head is on the floor.
   b. The bus driver's head is almost to the floor. ⟵ circled

4. a. Ramya tries to push the bus driver out of the driver's seat.
   b. Ramya tries to pull the bus driver out of the driver's seat. ⟵ circled

5. a. The bus driver is a small man.
   b. The bus driver is a big man. ⟵ circled

6. a. Ramya can't move him. ⟵ circled
   b. Ramya can move him.

UNDERSTANDING PRONOUNS

Who is it? What is it? Write the letter of your answer on the line.

1. *He* is a waiter. ___c___
2. Ramya can't move *him*. ___e___
3. Ramya puts his hands on *it*. ___a___
4. Ramya puts his left foot on *it*. ___b___
5. *It* takes the bus driver to the hospital. ___f___
6. *They* are all OK. ___d___

a. the steering wheel
b. the brake
c. Ramya
d. the passengers
e. the bus driver
f. the ambulance

4. DISCUSSION

Ramya takes the bus home. How do the people in your class get home? Do they take the bus? Do they take the subway? Do they drive? Do they walk? Do they ride a bike? Do they get a ride with someone?

Walk around the room. Ask five people the question below. Write each person's name in the chart. Then check (✔) each person's answer.

How do you get home?

Name	bus	subway	drive	walk	bike	ride with someone	other
1. _____	☐	☐	☐	☑	☐	☐	☐
2. _____	☑	☐	☐	☐	☐	☐	☐
3. _____	☐	☐	☑	☐	☐	☐	☐
4. _____	☑	☐	☐	☐	☐	☐	☐
5. _____	☑	☐	☐	☐	☐	☐	☐

5. WRITING

Make five sentences with the information in the discussion exercise. For example:

> Kanjana drives home.
>
> Alfredo gets a ride with Francisco.

Now write your sentences on your own paper.

1. PRE-READING

Look at the pictures. Listen to your teacher tell the story.

1

2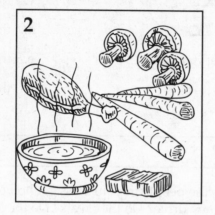

3

4

5

6

7

8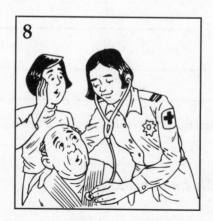

9

Grandfather Hada's Favorite Soup

IT is New Year's Day in Japan. The Hada family is eating a special New Year's soup. The soup has chicken, vegetables, and mochi in it. Mochi are rice cakes.

Grandfather Hada likes mochi. He takes a big bite of mochi. Then he begins to cough.

Grandfather Hada coughs and coughs. He can't stop coughing. The mochi is stuck in his throat.

Grandfather Hada's face is purple. He can't breathe. Someone runs to the phone and calls an ambulance. When will the ambulance arrive? Maybe in five or ten minutes. That will be too late.

Grandfather Hada's daughter gets the vacuum cleaner. She turns the vacuum cleaner on and turns the power to "high." She puts the vacuum cleaner hose into Grandfather Hada's throat. Whoosh! The mochi comes out of his throat and goes into the vacuum cleaner. Now Grandfather Hada can breathe.

Nine minutes later, the ambulance arrives, and paramedics check Grandfather Hada. He is fine.

Next year, on New Year's Day, the Hada family will eat a special soup. The soup will have chicken and vegetables in it. But it will have no mochi!

2. VOCABULARY

Write the correct word on the line.

stuck   check   breathe

bite   throat

1. Grandfather Hada loves to eat mochi. So he doesn't put a little mochi into his mouth.

   He opens his mouth and takes a big _____ bite _____.

2. The mochi goes into Grandfather's mouth. Then it goes down into his

   _____.

3. The mochi is in Grandfather Hada's throat. It doesn't go up, and it doesn't go down.

   It is _____.

4. Grandfather Hada's face is purple because no air is going into his body. He can't

   _____.

5. The paramedics examine Grandfather Hada. They listen to his heart, and they listen

   to his breathing. They _____ to see if he is OK.

3. COMPREHENSION

REMEMBERING DETAILS

One word in each sentence is not correct. Find the word and cross it out. Write the correct word.

1. It is New Year's Day in ~~China~~.   *Japan*

2. The Hada family is eating a special New Year's cake.

3. The soup has fish, vegetables, and mochi in it.

4. Mochi are potato cakes.

5. Grandfather Hada loves to make mochi.

6. The mochi is stuck in Grandfather Hada's tooth.

7. Grandfather Hada's face is white.

8. Next year, the New Year's soup will have no vegetables in it.

MAKING CONNECTIONS

Complete the sentences. Write the letter of your answer on the line.

1. Grandfather Hada takes a big bite of mochi

   and ___e___

2. Someone runs to the phone and _____

3. Grandfather Hada's daughter turns turns the vacuum

   cleaner on and _____

4. The mochi comes out of Grandfather Hada's

   throat and _____

5. Paramedics arrive and _____

a. turns the power to "high."

b. goes into the vacuum cleaner.

c. check Grandfather Hada.

d. calls an ambulance.

e. begins to cough.

4. DISCUSSION

Talk about your favorite foods. First, answer the questions. Write your answer on the line.

What do you like to eat? _____
(For example: I like to eat pizza.)

When do you like to eat it? _____
(For example: I like to eat it late at night.)

Tell your teacher your answers. Your teacher will make a list on the board. For example:

Who	What	When
Aldo	pizza	late at night
Adriana	ice cream	in the summer

Walk around the room. Tell your classmates about your favorite food and when you like to eat it.

5. WRITING

Make five sentences with the information on the board. For example:

> Aldo likes to eat pizza, and he eats it late at night.
>
> Adriana likes to eat ice cream, but she eats it only in the summer.

Now write your sentences on your own paper.

UNIT 6

1. PRE-READING

Look at the pictures. Listen to your teacher tell the story.

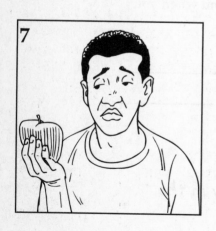

Handsome Again?

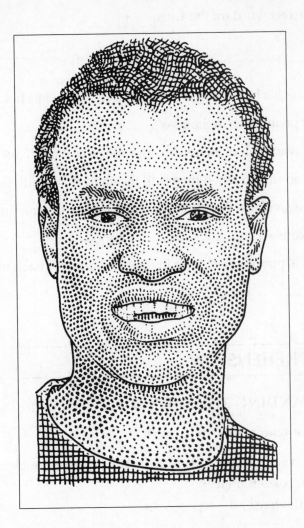

WHEN Santino Deng was ten years old, men in his village pulled six of his teeth out—the six bottom front teeth. Why?

In Santino's village in Sudan, in Africa, it is the custom. People there say, "Men with no front teeth look handsome. Women with no front teeth look beautiful."

So, when the children in Santino's village are ten years old, men pull their teeth out. The children do not cry. The boys want to look handsome. The girls want to look beautiful.

Now Santino has a problem. He is living in the United States. People in the United States think, "Men with no front teeth are not handsome. Women with no front teeth are not beautiful."

There is another problem. In Santino's village, all the food is soft. It is easy to eat with no front teeth. In the United States, not all the food is soft. It is not easy to eat apples and hamburgers with no front teeth.

A dentist is putting new teeth in Santino's mouth. It is expensive, and it is painful. But Santino wants the new teeth. "In Sudan, I was handsome," he says. "Here, I am not. I want to be handsome again."

2. VOCABULARY

Write the correct word on the line.

handsome   front   village
painful   expensive   soft

1. Santino has his back teeth, but he doesn't have six of his _____ *front* _____ teeth.

2. Only 400 people live in Santino's _____.

3. The girls want to look beautiful, and the boys want to look _____.

4. It hurts very much when men pull the children's teeth. It is _____.

5. In Santino's village, people eat cereal mixed with water or milk. It is easy to eat cereal because it is _____ food.

6. A dentist is putting new teeth in Santino's mouth. Each tooth costs $500. The new teeth are _____.

3. COMPREHENSION

UNDERSTANDING THE MAIN IDEAS

Complete the sentences. Circle *a* or *b*.

1. The men in Santino's village pulled six of his teeth out because
   (a.) it is the custom there.
   b. his teeth were bad.

2. The boys do not cry when men pull their teeth out because
   a. they want to look handsome.
   b. it is not painful.

3. It is not easy for Santino to eat in the United States because
   a. he doesn't like the food.
   b. not all the food is soft.

4. Santino wants new teeth because
   a. he wants to go back to his village with new teeth.
   b. he wants to be handsome again.

REVIEWING THE STORY

Write the correct word on the line.

When Santino Deng was ten years old, men in his village _____*pulled*_____

his bottom front teeth out. Why? It is the _____.

Now Santino is living in the United States. People there think he is not

_____. He has another problem: It is not easy to

_____ with no front teeth.

A _____ is putting new teeth in Santino's mouth. He wants

to be handsome _____.

4. DISCUSSION

Do you think these things look beautiful? Share your opinion with the class.

1. tattoos

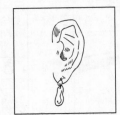

2. pierced ears

3. a pierced eyebrow

4. make-up

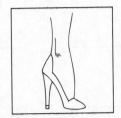

5. high heels

5. WRITING

Make five sentences with the information in the discussion exercise. For example:

I think tattoos do not look beautiful.

Now write your sentences on your own paper.

UNIT 7

1. PRE-READING

Look at the pictures. Listen to your teacher tell the story.

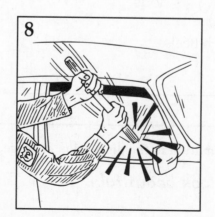

26   Unit 7

A Super Soaker and a Super Kid

DANIEL Ayala, ten years old, is walking down the street on a hot summer day. It is 92 degrees.[1] Daniel passes a parked car. He hears dogs barking, and he looks inside the car. Two puppies are in the car. The puppies look hot and thirsty. Daniel is worried about the puppies. "Maybe the puppies will die," he thinks.

Daniel tries to open the car doors, but they are locked. Daniel looks around. There are no people on the street. Nobody can help him.

Daniel runs home and gets his squirt gun. It is a big squirt gun—a "Super Soaker." It holds a lot of water. Daniel fills his squirt gun with cool water. Then he runs back to the car.

The car windows are open a little. Daniel squirts water at the puppies. He squirts water on their faces and into their mouths. For one hour, Daniel stands next to the car. Every five minutes, he squirts water at the puppies.

Finally, help comes. A police officer breaks a car window and opens a door. Daniel picks up the puppies. They are OK— thanks to Daniel and his Super Soaker.

[1]33.3 degrees Celsius

2. VOCABULARY

Write the correct word on the line.

fills	puppies	cool
worried	degrees	locked

1. It is very hot. The temperature is 92 _____ *degrees* _____.

2. The two dogs in the car are young. They are _____.

3. Daniel thinks, "Maybe the puppies will die." He is _____ about the puppies.

4. Daniel can't open the car doors. They are _____.

5. Daniel puts water in his squirt gun. He _____ it with water.

6. The water is cold but not very cold. It is _____.

3. COMPREHENSION

REMEMBERING DETAILS

Complete the sentences. Write your answer on the line.

1. Daniel is eight years old, right?

   No, he is _____ *ten years old* _____.

2. It is a cold winter day, right?

   No, it is a _____.

3. Three puppies are in the car, right?

   No, _____.

4. The puppies look hungry, right?

   No, they look _____.

5. Daniel stands next to the car for 20 minutes, right?

   No, he stands next to the car for _____.

6. A paramedic breaks a car window, right?

   No, a _____.

UNDERSTANDING PRONOUNS

Who is it? What is it? Write the letter of your answer on the line.

1. *He* squirts water at the puppies. ___d___
2. *They* look hot and thirsty. _____
3. *They* are locked. _____
4. Daniel fills *it* with cool water. _____
5. *They* are open a little. _____

a. his squirt gun

b. the car windows

c. the car doors

d. Daniel

e. the puppies

4. DISCUSSION

Imagine this: You are walking down the street on a hot summer day. You see two puppies in a locked car. The puppies look hot and thirsty. You do not have a squirt gun.

What do you do? Check (✔) your answer. Then explain your answer in a small group.

☐ call the police

☐ break a car window

☐ look for the puppies' owner

☐ do nothing

because _____

_____ .

5. WRITING

A. **Prepare for a dictation. Practice with the sentences below. Follow the directions on page 82.**

1. Walk down the street.
2. Look inside the car.
3. Try to open the car doors.
4. Look around.
5. Run home.
6. Fill your squirt gun with water.
7. Run back to the car.

B. **Now close your book. On your own paper, write the sentences as your teacher reads them. Then open your book and check your writing.**

1. PRE-READING

Look at the pictures. Listen to your teacher tell the story.

The Flying Lesson

BARBARA wants to be a pilot. She wants to fly a small airplane. "I want to take flying lessons," she tells her husband.

"Flying lessons?" her husband says. "Flying is dangerous!"

"Don't worry," Barbara says. "I'll be fine."

Barbara takes flying lessons. Today she is practicing landing. She is in a small airplane with her teacher. Barbara sees the airport. Then she sees the runway. She flies lower and lower. "Good!" her teacher says.

Barbara hears a loud noise on the top of the airplane. "What's that?" Barbara asks her teacher.

"I don't know!" the teacher says. "Land the plane, Barbara. Land the plane."

Barbara lands the airplane. She and her teacher get out of the airplane. They see another, bigger airplane. It is on top of their airplane.

The pilot gets out of the bigger airplane. "Sorry," the pilot says. "I was landing, too. I didn't see you."

Later Barbara goes home. "How was your flying lesson?" her husband asks.

"Fine," Barbara says. "Today I landed two airplanes—a small airplane and a bigger airplane."

"No problems?" her husband asks.

Barbara smiles. "No," she says. "No problems."

2. VOCABULARY

Write the correct word on the line.

landing   on top of   dangerous
noise   lessons   practicing

1. Barbara tells her husband, "I want to be a pilot." Her husband is worried. "Flying is _____*dangerous*_____!" he says.

2. Barbara wants to learn to fly an airplane. So, she pays a teacher $40 an hour to teach her. She takes flying _____*lesons*_____.

3. Barbara flies lower and lower because she is _____*landing*_____ the airplane.

4. Barbara lands the airplane. Then she lands it again and again. She is _____*practicing*_____ landing.

5. Barbara hears something. "What was that _____*noise*_____?" she asks her teacher.

6. The loud noise is not under the airplane. It is _____*on top of*_____ the airplane.

3. COMPREHENSION

REMEMBERING DETAILS

Complete the sentences. Write your answer on the line.

1. Barbara wants to be a mechanic, right?

   No, she wants to be a _____*pilot*_____.

2. She wants to fly a big airplane, right?

   No, she wants to fly a _____*small airplane,*_____.

3. The bigger airplane is under the small airplane, right?

   No, it is _____*on top of their airplane.*_____.

4. The pilot gets out of the bigger plane and says, "Hello," right?

   No, the pilot says, "_____*Sorry, I was landing to, I did't see ya.*_____."

5. Barbara tells her husband, "Today I landed three airplanes," right?

   No, she tells him, "Today I landed _____*two airplanes.*_____."

WHO SAYS IT?

Write the letter of your answer on the line.

1. "How was your flying lesson?" ___d___

2. "Land the plane, Barbara." ___b___

3. "I want to take flying lessons." ___a___

4. "Sorry. I was landing, too. I didn't see you." ___c___

a. Barbara

b. the teacher

c. the pilot of the bigger airplane

d. Barbara's husband

---

4. DISCUSSION

Barbara wants to fly a small airplane. And you? What do you want to do?

Draw a picture on your own paper. In the picture, you are doing what you want to do. Look at the example on the right.

Show your picture to a small group of classmates. Tell your classmates what you want to do.

---

5. WRITING

Tell your teacher what you want to do. Your teacher will make a list on the board. For example:

Kenji   sleep

Bujar   buy a computer

Make five sentences with the information on the board. For example:

Kenji wants to sleep.

Bujar wants to buy a computer.

Now write your sentences on your own paper.

1. PRE-READING

Look at the pictures. Listen to your teacher tell the story.

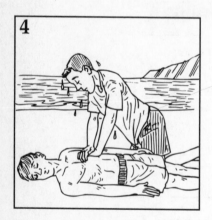

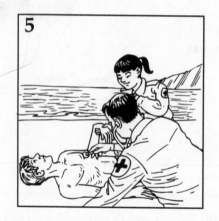

Hawaiian Vacation

QUENTIN Gwynn is in Hawaii with friends. He is on vacation, and he is having a wonderful time.

One afternoon Quentin is standing on a high rock. He is looking at the ocean. He sees a boy in the water below. The boy is in trouble. He is far from the beach, and he can't swim. Quentin takes off his backpack and his shoes. Then he jumps into the water, swims to the boy, and pulls him to the beach.

The boy isn't breathing. Quentin gives him CPR, and the boy begins to breathe again. Later, an ambulance comes. Paramedics check the boy. "He is fine," the paramedics tell Quentin. "You saved his life."

Quentin walks back to the high rock. His shoes are there, but his backpack is gone. Quentin's credit cards, his camera, and his money were in the backpack. "Well," Quentin thinks, "this is the end of my vacation."

Quentin's story is in the newspaper. People read about Quentin and the boy. They also read about Quentin's backpack.

A hotel owner tells Quentin, "Your room here is free." Restaurant owners tell Quentin, "Your meals here are free." A lot of people give Quentin money. "Here's money for a new camera," the people say. "Buy some other things, too. Have fun in Hawaii."

So it is not the end of Quentin's vacation. He stays in Hawaii an extra week. He has a wonderful time.

2. VOCABULARY

Write the correct word on the line.

free	gone	credit card
meals	CPR	in trouble

1. The boy in the water is far from the beach, and he can't swim. That is dangerous.

   Quentin sees that the boy is _____ in trouble _____.

2. Quentin pushes on the boy's chest five times. Then he breathes into the boy's mouth.

   He does this many times. Quentin is giving the boy _____ CPR _____.

3. When Quentin goes back to the high rock, his backpack is not there. It is

   _____ gone _____.

4. When Quentin buys something, he doesn't always pay with cash. Sometimes he pays

   with a _____ credit card _____.

5. Quentin doesn't pay for his hotel room. It is _____ free _____.

6. Quentin doesn't pay for his breakfast, lunch, or dinner. All his

   _____ meals _____ are free, too.

3. COMPREHENSION

UNDERSTANDING THE MAIN IDEAS

Answer the questions. Circle *a* or *b*.

1. Where is Quentin?
   - **a.** He is on vacation in Hawaii.
   - **b.** He is on vacation in Mexico.

2. Who gives the boy CPR?
   - **a.** Paramedics give the boy CPR.
   - **b.** Quentin gives the boy CPR.

3. What happens to Quentin's backpack?
   - **a.** Someone takes it.
   - **b.** He leaves it at the hotel.

4. What is in Quentin's backpack?
   - **a.** His credit cards, his camera, and his money are in his backpack.
   - **b.** His sunglasses, his camera, and a map of Hawaii are in his backpack.

5. What do people give Quentin?
   - **a.** They give him a free plane ticket home.
   - **b.** They give him a free hotel room, free meals, and money.

UNDERSTANDING SEQUENCE

Which happens first? Write 1 on the line. Which happens second? Write 2 on the line.

1. Quentin pulls the boy to the beach.   2

   Quentin jumps into the water.   1

2. Quentin gives the boy CPR.   _____

   The boy begins to breathe again.   _____

3. Paramedics tell Quentin the boy is fine.   _____

   An ambulance comes.   _____

4. Someone takes Quentin's backpack.   _____

   Quentin's story is in the newspaper.   _____

5. People give Quentin money.   _____

   Quentin stays in Hawaii an extra week.   _____

4. DISCUSSION / WRITING

What are some good places for a vacation? Is Hawaii a good place? Is Acapulco, Mexico, a good place? Is Paris, France, a good place?

Talk about and write about good places for a vacation. Follow these steps:

A. With your classmates, make a list of good places for a vacation. Write your list on the board.

B. Choose one of the places on the board. On your own paper, write four sentences about it. (Do not write the name of the place on your paper.) For example:

> 1. It is hot there.
>
> 2. There are beautiful beaches.
>
> 3. Many people go there to see the sunset.
>
> 4. Young men dive into the ocean from high rocks.

C. Tape your paper to a wall in your classroom.

D. Walk around the room. Read the sentences on each paper. Which place do the sentences describe? If you think you know, write the place on the paper.

E. Take your paper off the wall and read your sentences to the class. Tell the class the name of the place you described.

UNIT 10

1. PRE-READING

Look at the pictures. Listen to your teacher tell the story.

Election Day

HERB Casey wants to be mayor of his city. So he works hard. He puts up signs. "VOTE FOR HERB CASEY" the signs say. He knocks on doors and talks to people. "Please vote for me," he says. He mails letters to thousands of people. "Please vote for me," he writes. He gives speeches. "Vote for me!" he says in his speeches.

Finally, it is Election Day. It is time for people to vote. Herb works extra hard on Election Day. He puts up more signs and knocks on more doors. He calls people on the phone, too. "Today is Election Day," he says. "Please vote for me."

At eight o'clock in the evening, Herb stops making phone calls and goes to vote. It is ten minutes after eight when Herb arrives to vote. He is too late. Voting stops at eight o'clock. Herb cannot vote.

The next day, people count the votes. Is Herb Casey the new mayor? Does he win the election? No, he doesn't. He loses the election by one vote.

2. VOCABULARY

Match the words and the pictures. Write your answer on the line.

5 vote   2 knock on doors   4 mail letters
1 put up signs 6 call people on the phone 3 give speeches

1. ___put up signs___   2. _____   3. _____

4. ____2?____   5. _____   6. _____

3. COMPREHENSION

UNDERSTANDING THE MAIN IDEAS

Complete the sentences. Circle the letter of your answer.

1. Herb works hard because
   a. he wants to be president of his country.
   b. he wants to be mayor of his city.
   c. he wants to be rich.

2. Herb loses the election because
   a. he doesn't put up signs.
   b. people don't like him.
   c. he doesn't vote.

3. Herb doesn't vote because
   a. he knows he will win the election.
   b. he arrives too late to vote.
   c. he is not in his city on election day.

REMEMBERING DETAILS

Herb works hard because he wants to be mayor of his city. What does he do?
Check (✔) five answers.

☑ He gives speeches.

☑ He gives people money.

☐ He puts up signs.

☑ He calls people on the phone.

☐ He mails letters.

☑ He puts his picture in the newspaper.

☑ He knocks on doors and talks to people.

☐ He votes many times.

4. DISCUSSION

Circle *yes* or *no*. Then share your answers with the class.

In my country, people who want to win an election . . .

1. put up signs.	YES	NO ✔
2. mail letters.	YES	NO
3. knock on doors.	YES ✔	NO
4. give speeches.	YES ✔	NO
5. call people on the phone.	YES	NO ✔
6. _____		
(other)		

5. WRITING

Think about people who want to win an election in your country. What do they do?
What don't they do?

Make five sentences with the information in the discussion exercise. For example:

They put up signs.

They don't mail letters.

Now write your sentences on your own paper.

1. PRE-READING

Look at the pictures. Listen to your teacher tell the story.

The Best Doctor

CONNIE is having trouble with her knee. Her knee hurts, and she walks with a limp. Her doctor tells her, "You need surgery on your knee." So Connie has surgery.

After the surgery, Connie's knee feels better. It doesn't hurt. But she still walks with a limp. Connie goes to many doctors. "Please help me," Connie says. "I don't want to walk with a limp." But the doctors can't help Connie. She still walks with a limp.

One morning Connie is walking to work when she sees something big and brown. What is it? Is it an animal? Yes, it is! It is a bear, and it is running toward Connie.

Connie lives in Alaska. In Alaska, bears come into the city sometimes. The bears are dangerous. They can kill people.

Connie runs toward a building, and the bear runs after her. The bear runs fast, and Connie runs fast, too; she doesn't think about her knee. Connie runs into the building and closes the door. The bear stands outside and growls.

Connie walks to a phone to call the police. She does not walk with a limp.

Connie never walks with a limp again, and she never has another problem with her knee. Connie went to many doctors, but the bear was the best doctor!

2. VOCABULARY

Write the correct word on the line.

dangerous	surgery	limp
trouble	hurts	toward

1. Connie has a problem: She is having _____ *trouble* _____ with her knee.

2. "Ow!" Connie says when she walks. Her knee _____.

3. Connie can't walk fast because she walks with a _____.

4. Connie goes to a hospital and has _____ on her knee.

5. Connie can see the bear's face because it is running in her direction. It is running _____ Connie.

6. Bears sometimes kill people. They are _____.

3. COMPREHENSION

MAKING CONNECTIONS

Complete the sentences. Write the letter of your answer on the line.

1. Connie is having trouble __ *e* __   a. into a building.

2. She walks_____   b. into the city.

3. Connie lives _____   c. in Alaska.

4. Sometimes bears come _____   d. toward Connie.

5. The bear runs _____   e. with her knee.

6. Connie runs _____   f. with a limp.

REVIEWING THE STORY

Write the correct word on the line.

Connie's knee hurts and she _____ *walks* _____ with a limp, so she has
[1]

surgery. After the surgery, Connie's knee doesn't hurt, but she _____
[2]

walks with a limp.

One day Connie is walking to _____ when a
[3]

_____ runs after her. Connie runs fast. She runs into a
[4]

_____. Connie never limps again, and she never has another
[5]

problem with her _____ .
[6]

---

4. DISCUSSION

Talk about going to the doctor in the United States and in your country.

Answer the questions below. In a small group, take a guess. Write your group's answer on the line. Then share your group's answers with the class. (The correct answers are on page 82.)

1. How many times a year do people
   in the United States go to the doctor?[1]   _____ times a year

2. When people go to a doctor in the United States,
   how many minutes are they with the doctor?   _____ minutes

3. How much does it cost to see a doctor
   in the United States? $_____

4. When people go to the emergency room at a hospital
   in the United States, how much does it cost? $_____

---

5. WRITING

Complete the sentences. Then copy the sentences on your own paper.

1. I go to the doctor _____ times a year.

2. I am with the doctor _____ minutes.

3. In my country, it costs _____ to see a doctor.

4. In my country, it costs _____ to go to the emergency room at a hospital.

---

[1]Look on page 82 to see how many times a year people in other countries go to the doctor.

1. PRE-READING

Look at the pictures. Listen to your teacher tell the story.

The Bottle

AKE Viking is a young sailor. He is on a ship near Sweden. There is nothing to do on the ship, and Ake is bored. Ake writes this letter in English:

> Are you a young woman, 16 to 20 years old?
> Do you want to marry a handsome young Swede?
> Please write me.
>
> Ake Viking

Ake writes his address on the letter. Then he puts the letter in a bottle and throws the bottle into the sea.

Two years later, Sebastiano Puzzo is fishing near his home in Italy. He sees a bottle in the water. He takes the bottle out of the water and opens it. Inside the bottle, he finds Ake's letter.

Sebastiano takes the letter home to his daughter. Her name is Paolina, and she is 18 years old. Sebastiano and Paolina read the letter and laugh.

Just for fun, Paolina writes a letter to Ake. She sends him a photo, too.

Ake reads Paolina's letter and writes a letter to her. Then she writes a letter to him. For one year, Ake and Paolina write letters. Ake doesn't know Italian, and Paolina doesn't know Swedish, so they write in English.

In one letter, Ake writes:

> Dear Paolina,
> I want to meet you. Is it OK if I visit you in Italy?
>
> Ake

Paolina writes that it is OK, so Ake goes to Italy. He meets Paolina and her family. Two months later, Paolina marries the handsome young Swede.

2. VOCABULARY

Match the words and the pictures. Write your answer on the line.

4 bottle
1 sailor

5 throw
6 sea

2 ship
3 address

Ake Viking
Odengatan 63
SE-114 Stockolm

1. _____ sailor _____   2. _____   3. _____

4. _____   5. _____   6. _____

3. COMPREHENSION

REMEMBERING DETAILS

1. Ake is on a ship near Spain, right?

   No, he is on a ship near _____ Sweden _____.

2. There is a lot to do on the ship, right?

   No, there is _____ nutingg _____.

3. Paolina is 21 years old, right?

   No, she is _____ 18 years old _____.

4. Ake and Paolina write for three years, right?

   No, they write for _____ one years, _____.

5. They write their letters in Italian, right?

   No, they write in _____ English _____.

MAKING CONNECTIONS

Complete the sentences. Write the letter of your answer on the line.

1. Ake puts his letter in a bottle and ___d___

2. Sebastiano Puzzo takes the bottle out of the water and ___c___

3. Sebastiano and Paolina read the letter and ___a___

4. Ake reads Paolina's letter and ___b___

a. laugh.

b. writes a letter to her.

c. brings it home to his daughter.

d. throws it into the sea.

4. DISCUSSION

Ake is from Sweden, and Paolina is from Italy. Ake doesn't speak Italian, and Paolina doesn't speak Swedish. When they talk, they speak English. Will they be happy together? What do you think?

If you think Ake and Paolina will be happy, put your X on the line near *YES*. If you think they will not be happy, put your X on the line near *NO*. If your answer is somewhere between *YES* and *NO*, put your X on the line between *YES* and *NO*. Then explain your answer in a small group.

Will Ake and Paolina be happy together?

NO ————————————————————————YES

5. WRITING

Imagine this: You want to write a letter, put your letter in a bottle, and throw the bottle into the sea. What will you write? Make a list of possible sentences. Write the sentences on the board. For example:

- *If you find this letter, please write me.*

- *You can write me in English or Chinese.*

- *My address is: 303 Center Street, Whitewater, WI 53190, USA*

- *I am single.*

Now write your letter on your own paper.

1. PRE-READING

Look at the pictures. Listen to your teacher tell the story.

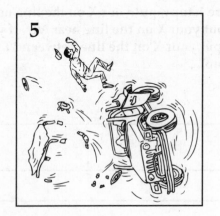

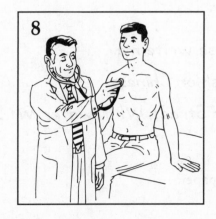

Hold On, Joe

JOE Thompson is 18 years old, and he drives a small Jeep. Joe loves to drive his car. Sometimes he wears his seat belt. Sometimes he doesn't.

One day Joe is driving his Jeep. He is not wearing his seat belt. Suddenly another car turns in front of him. Joe hits the other car. Joe's Jeep rolls over once, twice, three times, four times. The fourth time the Jeep rolls over, the top comes off. Joe goes up into the air. He goes up high.

There are some wires above the street. One wire catches Joe's foot. He grabs another wire with his hand. Now Joe is hanging high above the street. He is holding onto the wires. Joe is lucky: These wires are not for electricity; they are for telephones.

Joe has a cell phone in his pocket. He calls 911. Then he calls his father. "I had an accident," he tells his father. "I'm hanging from some wires high above the street." "Hold on, Joe," his father says. "Hold on."

Twenty minutes later, rescue workers take Joe down from the wires. Then they take him to the hospital. A doctor at the hospital tells Joe, "You are fine—no cuts, no broken bones. You can go home."

A few weeks later, Joe buys a new Jeep. He loves to drive his car. He always wears his seat belt.

2. VOCABULARY

Match the words and the pictures. Write your answer on the line.

roll over   hold on   hang
grab   turn   hit

1. _____turn_____   2. _____   3. _____

4. _____   5. _____   6. _____

3. COMPREHENSION

MAKING CONNECTIONS

Complete the sentences. Write the letter of your answer on the line.

1. Another car turns __c__
2. Joe goes up __e__
3. Joe has a cell phone __a__
4. Joe is hanging __d__
5. Rescue workers take Joe __b__

a. in his pocket.

b. to the hospital.

c. in front of Joe.

d. from some wires above the street.

e. into the air.

UNDERSTANDING SEQUENCE

Which happens first? Write 1 on the line. Which happens second? Write 2 on the line.

1. Joe hits the car. ___2___

   A car turns in front of Joe. ___1___

2. The Jeep rolls over once, twice, three times, four times. _____

   The top comes off the Jeep. _____

3. Joe grabs a wire with his hand. _____

   Joe goes up into the air. _____

4. Joe calls his father. _____

   Joe calls 911. _____

4. DISCUSSION

Walk around the room. Ask five people the question below. Write each person's name on the line. Check (✔) their answers.

Do you wear a seat belt?

Name	Always	Usually	Never
1. _____			
2. _____			
3. _____			
4. _____			
5. _____			

5. WRITING

Make sentences with the information from the discussion exercise. For example:

Jingjing always wears a seat belt.

Aldo usually wears a seat belt.

Mary never wears a seat belt.

Now write your sentences on your own paper.

1. PRE-READING

Look at the pictures. Listen to your teacher tell the story.

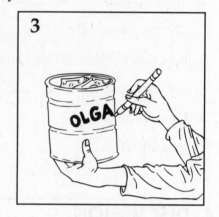

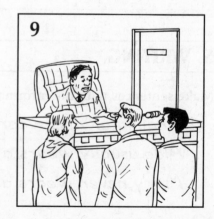

Whose Money Is It?

LOUISE Stamberg likes to save money. But she doesn't like banks. So she doesn't put her money in banks. She hides it in her house. She puts her money in cans. Then she puts the cans above the ceiling in her kitchen.

Louise writes "Olga" on some cans of money. Olga is Louise's niece. "This money is for Olga," Louise thinks. Louise doesn't tell Olga about the money. She doesn't tell anyone about the money.

When she is an old woman, Louise Stamberg dies. Then her niece Olga moves into Louise's house. Olga lives in the house for many years. Then she sells the house to Brian Williams.

Mr. Williams wants to remodel the kitchen. He hires a carpenter to do the work. The carpenter is fixing the ceiling when he finds 12 cans. He opens the cans, and what does he find? He finds money—a lot of money. He finds $150,000.

"It's my money!" the carpenter says. "I found it!"

"No, it's not your money," Mr. Williams says. "This is my house, so it's my money."

"No, it's not your money," Olga says. "The name 'Olga' is on some of the cans. I am Olga, so it's my money."

A judge must decide: Whose money is it? Is it the carpenter's money? Is it Mr. Williams' money? Or is it Olga's money? What does the judge decide? What do you think?

2. VOCABULARY

Write the correct word on the line.

ceiling	hides	judge
hires	remodel	found

1. Louise Stamberg doesn't want people to find her money. So, she

   _____ *hides* _____ it.

2. When Olga sits in her kitchen and looks up, she doesn't see the cans of money. She

   sees only the _____.

3. The kitchen in Mr. Williams' house is old. He wants to paint the kitchen, fix the

   ceiling, and buy a new refrigerator. He wants to _____ the
   kitchen.

4. Mr. Williams asks a carpenter, "Can you remodel my kitchen? I'll pay you $20 an
   hour to do the work." The carpenter says, "Yes, I'll do the work." Mr. Williams

   _____ the carpenter.

5. The carpenter finds the money above the ceiling. Later he says, "It is my money

   because I _____ it."

6. Whose money is it? Olga, Mr. Williams, and the carpenter go to court. They want

   a _____ to decide.

3. COMPREHENSION

UNDERSTANDING THE MAIN IDEAS

Answer the questions. Circle *a* or *b*.

1. Why does Louise Stamberg hide money in her house?
   a. She is sick and can't go to the bank.
   b. She doesn't like banks.

2. Where does Louise hide the money?
   a. She hides it above the ceiling in her kitchen.
   b. She hides it under the floor in her kitchen.

3. What does Louise write on some cans of money?
   a. She writes the name "Olga."
   b. She writes, "Do not open."

4. Who is Olga?

    a. She is Louise Stamberg's sister.

    b. She is Louise Stamberg's niece.

5. How does the carpenter find the money?

    a. He finds it when he is fixing the ceiling.

    b. He finds it when he is putting new lights in the kitchen.

WHO SAYS IT?

Who says it? Write the letter of your answer on the line.

1. "I found it, so it's my money." ___d___   **a.** Olga

2. "This money is for Olga." _____   **b.** Louise Stamberg

3. "This is my house, so it's my money." _____   **c.** Mr. Williams

4. "My name is on some of the cans, so it's my money." _____   **d.** the carpenter

4. DISCUSSION

Imagine this: You are the judge. Whose money is it? What do you decide? Check (✔) your answer. Then explain your answer in a small group. (Look on page 82 to see what the judge decided.)

☐ All the money is for Olga.

☐ All the money is for Mr. Williams.

☐ All the money is for the carpenter.

☐ Some of the money is for _____, and some of the money is for

_____.

5. WRITING

A. Prepare for a dictation. Practice with the sentences below. Follow the directions on page 82.

1. Put the money in cans.
2. Write "Olga" on the cans.
3. Put the cans above the ceiling.
4. Fix the ceiling.
5. Open the cans.

B. Now close your book. On your own paper, write the sentences as your teacher says them. Then open your book and check your writing.

UNIT 15

1. PRE-READING

Look at the pictures. Listen to your teacher tell the story.

1

2
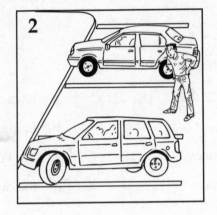

3

4

5

6

7

8

9

The Silver Porsche

TOSHI lives in Tokyo, Japan. But he doesn't drive a Japanese car. He drives a German car—a 2003 Porsche. It is a silver sports car, and it is almost new. It has only 15,000 kilometers on it. Toshi loves his car!

One day a thief steals Toshi's car. Toshi is angry. He wants his car back! Toshi thinks about his car. Where is it? Is the thief driving it? Probably not. Probably the thief sold it—maybe to a used-car dealer.

Toshi goes to his computer and gets on the Internet. He clicks on "Shop: Autos." Then he clicks on "Used Cars."

Toshi types in "Porsche" and "Tokyo." He gets 92 hits: Used-car dealers in Tokyo have 92 Porsches for sale.

Next, Toshi types in "Year: 2003." He gets 20 hits: Used-car dealers in Tokyo have 20 2003 Porsches for sale.

Then Toshi types in "Color: silver." He gets four hits: Used-car dealers in Tokyo have four silver 2003 Porsches for sale.

Finally, Toshi types in "with 15,000 kilometers." He gets one hit: Only one used-car dealer in Tokyo has a silver 2003 Porsche with 15,000 kilometers on it.

Toshi goes to the used-car dealer and looks at the silver Porsche. Toshi remembers that his car has a small scratch. Does this car have a small scratch? Yes, it does! This is Toshi's car. He is sure of it. He calls the police.

Two days later, Toshi is driving his silver Porsche again.

2. VOCABULARY

Match the words and the pictures. Write your answer on the line.

type   click on   thief
used-car dealer   scratch   hits

1. _____thief_____ 2. _____ 3. _____

4. _____ 5. _____ 6. _____

3. COMPREHENSION

REMEMBERING DETAILS

Complete the sentences. Write your answer on the line.

1. Toshi lives in Sydney, Australia, right?

   No, he lives in _____Tokyo, Japan_____.

2. Toshi drives a Japanese car, right?

   No, he drives a _____.

3. Toshi's car is black, right?

   No, it is _____.

4. The car has 5,000 kilometers on it, right?

   No, it has _____.

5. Toshi thinks the thief is probably driving his car, right?

   No, he thinks the thief probably _____.

REVIEWING THE STORY

Write the correct word on the line.

A thief steals Toshi's car, and he is _____*angry*_____. He wants his car

_____.
             2

He goes to his computer and _____ the Internet. He clicks on
                                          3

"_____: Autos." Then he clicks on "_____
            4   5

Cars." He finds a silver 2003 Porsche with 15,000 _____. A
                                                                          6

used-car dealer has it.

Toshi goes to the used-car dealer and looks at the car. The car has a small scratch.

Toshi's car has a small scratch, so he is _____ this is his car. He
                                                          7

calls the _____.
                    8

Two days _____, Toshi is driving his silver Porsche again.
                        9

4. DISCUSSION

Which cars do thieves in the United States like to steal?

**Look at the list below. Which two cars are the most popular with thieves? In a small
group, take a guess. Circle the names of two cars. Then tell the class your group's
answer.** (The correct answer is on page 82.)

Ford	Honda	Mercedes	Toyota
Chevrolet	Jeep	BMW	Hyundai
Lincoln	Cadillac	Volkswagen	Porsche

5. WRITING

Circle *want* or *don't want*. Then complete the sentences on your own paper. For example:

I want / don't want a sports car because *I have a big family.*

1. I want / don't want a sports car because . . .

2. I want / don't want a silver car because . . .

3. I want / don't want a used car because . . .

4. I want / don't want a computer because . . .

1. PRE-READING

Look at the pictures. Listen to your teacher tell the story.

An Easy Job

ANNE wants to put new vinyl on her kitchen floor. It is a small floor, so Anne thinks, "This is an easy job. I can do it myself. "

First, Anne spreads glue on the floor. Then she carries in the vinyl. Whoops! She falls down. She falls right into the glue. The glue is on Anne's hands and legs, but Anne doesn't stop to clean it off. "I can clean the glue off later," Anne thinks. She wants to put down the vinyl before the glue on the floor dries. Quickly, Anne puts the vinyl on the floor. It looks great. "That was easy!" Anne thinks.

Now Anne remembers the glue on her hands and legs. How can she take it off? She sits down and calls a friend. "Do you know how to clean off glue?" she asks her friend.

"Sorry," her friend says. "I don't know."

"Well, thanks anyway," Anne says. "Bye."

When she finishes talking, Anne tries to hang up the phone. She can't. Her right hand is glued to the phone. Then she tries to stand up. She can't. Her legs are glued to the chair. Anne needs help. She tries to dial 911 with her left hand. She can't. Her left hand is glued to her left leg. She dials 911 with her nose.

Firefighters arrive. Firefighters usually fight fires—they don't usually fight glue. But they know what to do. They have a special cleaner. It takes off glue. Three firefighters clean the glue off Anne. It takes them one hour. It is not an easy job!

2. VOCABULARY

Write the correct word on the line.

Thanks anyway	myself	hang up
quickly	take off	spreads

1. Anne thinks, "This is an easy job. I don't need help. I can do it

   _____ myself _____."

2. Anne puts the glue everywhere on the floor. She _____ the glue.

3. Anne works fast. She puts the vinyl on the floor _____.

4. Anne doesn't want glue on her hands and legs. She wants to

   _____ the glue.

5. Anne's friend has no information about cleaning off glue. So Anne doesn't say,

   "Thank you for your help." She says, " _____."

6. When Anne finishes her conversation, she wants to _____ the phone.

3. COMPREHENSION

UNDERSTANDING THE MAIN IDEAS

Answer the questions. Circle _a_ or _b_.

1. What job does Anne want to do?
   a. She wants to put new vinyl on her kitchen floor.
   b. She wants to paint her kitchen.

2. Why does Anne think, "This is an easy job"?
   a. It is a small floor.
   b. Anne works with vinyl every day.

3. Who comes to clean the glue off Anne?
   a. Firefighters come.
   b. Anne's friends come.

4. How long does it take to clean off the glue?
   a. It takes three hours.
   b. It takes one hour.

FINDING MORE INFORMATION

Read each sentence on the left. Which sentence on the right gives you more information? Match the sentences. Write the letter of your answer on the line.

1. Anne wants to put new vinyl on her kitchen floor. __d__

2. Anne falls down. _____

3. Anne calls a friend. _____

4. The firefighters have a special cleaner. _____

5. The firefighters clean the glue off Anne. _____

a. It takes off glue.

b. It takes them one hour.

c. "Do you know how to clean off glue?" she asks.

d. It is a small floor.

e. She falls right into the glue.

4. DISCUSSION

What jobs can you do in your house? With your classmates, make a list. Your teacher will write your list on the board. For example:

Kai   put vinyl on the floor

Yumiko   paint

Now sit with a partner. Use the information on the board to ask your partner questions. For example:

Can you paint? Yes, I can.   OR   No, I can't. But Yumiko can.

5. WRITING

Make five sentences with the information on the board. For example:

Kai can put vinyl on the floor.

Yumiko can paint.

Now write your sentences on your own paper.

1. PRE-READING

Look at the pictures. Listen to your teacher tell the story.

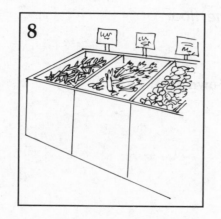

The Pet Rabbit

MRS. Nunn is at the supermarket with her three children. She looks worried. Her husband has no work, and she has only a little money for food.

A young man is working at the supermarket. His name is Jeff. Jeff is throwing old vegetables into a box. "What are you going to do with those vegetables?" Mrs. Nunn asks.

"I'm going to throw them in the garbage," Jeff says.

"Can I have them?" Mrs. Nunn asks. "We have a pet rabbit. I can give the vegetables to the rabbit."

"Sure, you can have the vegetables," Jeff says. He gives Mrs. Nunn a big box of old vegetables.

The Nunn family doesn't really have a pet rabbit. Mrs. Nunn wants the old vegetables to make soup for her family.

Every week Jeff gives Mrs. Nunn a box of vegetables for the "rabbit." Sometimes Mrs. Nunn finds cans of soup under the vegetables. Sometimes she finds soap, juice, or baby food.

When Mrs. Nunn goes to the supermarket one day, Jeff is not there. He doesn't work at the supermarket anymore. But It doesn't matter. Mrs. Nunn's husband is working again. She doesn't need the old vegetables.

Ten years go by. Mrs. Nunn is shopping at the supermarket when she sees Jeff. He is standing in the store's office. He is the store manager now.

"Mrs. Nunn!" Jeff says. "I think of you and your family often." Then he asks quietly, "How is the rabbit?"

"Thank you for asking," Mrs. Nunn says and smiles. "The rabbit left a long time ago. We are all doing fine."

2. VOCABULARY

Write the correct word on the line.

| manager | worried | it doesn't matter |
| anymore | quietly | pet |

1. Mrs. Nunn is thinking, "My children are hungry. But I have only a little money. How can I buy food for my children?" She is _____ *worried* _____.

2. Mrs. Nunn says, "We have a rabbit. It lives in our house. It is a _____ rabbit."

3. Jeff has a new job now. He works at a different place. He doesn't work at the supermarket _____.

4. One day Mrs. Nunn goes to the supermarket, and Jeff is not there. There are no boxes of vegetables for her, but it is not a problem. Her husband is working now, so _____.

5. Ten years later, Mrs. Nunn goes to the supermarket and sees Jeff. He is a boss at the supermarket. He is the store _____.

6. Jeff doesn't want other people to hear his conversation with Mrs. Nunn. So he asks _____, "How is the rabbit?"

3. COMPREHENSION

UNDERSTANDING THE MAIN IDEAS

Answer the questions. Circle *a* or *b*.

1. Who is Jeff?
   a. He is Mrs. Nunn's husband.
   b. He is a young man who works at the supermarket.

2. Why is Jeff throwing old vegetables into a box?
   a. He is going to give them to poor people.
   b. He is going to throw them in the garbage.

3. Why does Mrs. Nunn want the old vegetables?
   a. She wants to sell them.
   b. She wants to make soup.

4. Why does Mrs. Nunn say, "I can give the vegetables to the rabbit"?
   a. She doesn't want Jeff to know the vegetables are for her family.
   b. She has a pet rabbit, and the rabbit is always hungry.

5. Why does Jeff put soup, soap, juice, and baby food under the vegetables?

    a. He knows rabbits like these things.

    b. He knows Mrs. Nunn needs these things for her family.

UNDERSTANDING DIALOG

Match the questions and the answers. Write the letter of your answer on the line.

1. "What are you going to do with those vegetables?" ___c___

2. "Can I have the old vegetables?" _____

3. "How is the rabbit?" _____

4. "How are you and your family?" _____

a. "Sure, you can have them."

b. "Thank you for asking. We are all doing fine."

c. "I'm going to throw them in the garbage."

d. "It left a long time ago."

4. WRITING

When people have only a little money, they can't buy expensive food.

Think about a dinner that is delicious but not expensive. On your own paper, draw a picture of it. Look at the example on the right.

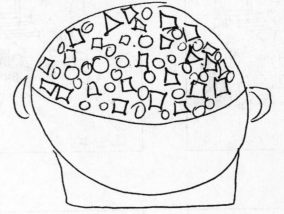

Under your picture, write three sentences about the dinner. For example:

- *This is a salad.*
- *It is potatoes, carrots, corn, and tuna mixed together with mayonnaise.*
- *It is good in hot weather.*

5. DISCUSSION

Show your picture to a partner. Tell your partner about the delicious dinner.

1. PRE-READING

Look at the pictures. Listen to your teacher tell the story.

The Birthday Present

JOE is shopping. He is looking for a present for his wife. Her birthday is in two days.

He sees a coat. It is a warm coat, and it is beautiful. It is also expensive—$1,000. Joe is not a rich man. But he loves the coat, and he loves his wife, so he buys the coat.

Joe doesn't want his wife to see the coat, so he puts it in a black plastic bag. Then he takes the coat to his brother's house.

When Joe arrives at his brother's house, his sister-in-law is outside shoveling snow. "I'll help you," Joe says. He puts the black plastic bag down on the snow.

While Joe is shoveling snow, a garbage truck comes. The men see the black plastic bag on the snow. They pick it up and throw it into the truck.

When Joe finishes shoveling the snow, he looks for the black plastic bag. It is gone! Then Joe remembers the garbage truck. "Oh, no!" he thinks. "Maybe the black plastic bag is in the garbage truck!"

The garbage truck takes garbage to the dump. So Joe drives to the dump. There are thousands of black plastic bags at the dump. Which one has the coat in it? For hours, Joe opens black plastic bags. He finds empty boxes and cans. He finds old shoes and clothes. He finds old potatoes and onions. Finally, he finds the coat.

Joe gives the coat to his wife on her birthday. "It's beautiful!" she says. "I love it! But . . ."

"But what?" Joe asks.

"It smells like onions."

2. VOCABULARY

Write the correct word on the line.

dump   present   gone
shoveling snow   empty   sister-in-law

1. Joe wants to give his wife something. He is looking for a _____ **present** _____ for her.

2. Joe's brother is married. When Joe arrives at his brother's house, his brother's wife is outside working. Joe helps his _____.

3. It is a cold winter day, and Joe's sister-in-law is _____.

4. Joe looks everywhere for the black plastic bag, but he can't find it. The bag is

   _____.

5. The garbage trucks take all the garbage to the _____.

6. Joe finds boxes and cans with nothing in them. They are _____.

3. COMPREHENSION

UNDERSTANDING THE MAIN IDEAS

Complete the sentences. Circle *a* or *b*.

1. Joe is looking for a present for his wife because
   a. she is in the hospital.
   b. her birthday is in two days.

2. Joe buys the expensive coat because
   a. he loves his wife.
   b. he is a rich man.

3. Joe puts the coat in a black plastic bag because
   a. he doesn't want the coat to get dirty.
   b. he doesn't want his wife to see it.

4. Joe doesn't see the garbage truck because
   a. he is watching TV.
   b. he is shoveling snow.

5. The coat smells like onions because
   a. it was at the garbage dump.
   b. Joe's wife is cooking onions.

REMEMBERING DETAILS

What does Joe find at the dump? Circle seven words.

(empty boxes)   old shoes   an old chair
old onions   empty cans   old clothes
an old bicycle   old potatoes   the coat

4. DISCUSSION / WRITING

Give a "present" to someone in your class.

- With your classmates, make a list of presents people like to give and receive. Your teacher will write your list on the board.

- Write your name on a small piece of paper. Put the piece of paper in a box. Your classmates will put their names in the box, too. Then reach into the box and take a name. You are going to give that person a "present."

- Choose a present from the list on the board. Then copy this letter on your own paper. Complete the letter as you copy it. Then fold your letter and deliver it to your classmate.

Dear _____,

I want to give you _____ for a present because
_____.

Your friend,

_____

Write a thank-you note for your present.

- When you return to your desk, you will find a "present" from a classmate on your desk. Write a thank-you note to the person who gave you the present.

- Copy the thank-you note below on your own paper. Complete the note as you copy it.

- Then fold your note and deliver it to the person who gave you the present.

Dear _____,

Thank you very much for _____. I liked the

present because _____.

Your friend,

_____

1. PRE-READING

Look at the pictures. Listen to your teacher tell the story.

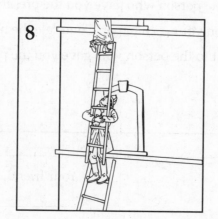

The Fire

"**F**IRE! Fire!"
It is 1873. The St. James Hotel in Montreal, Canada, is on fire.

Johanna O'Connor, 20 years old, works at the hotel. During the day, she works in the kitchen. At night, she sleeps in her room on the fifth floor.

Johanna is sleeping in her room when she hears people yelling, "Fire! Fire!" She runs to the door and opens it. She sees only black smoke. She closes the door, quickly gets dressed, and runs to the window.

"Help! Help!" she yells from the window.

Firefighters are on the street below. They see Johanna at the window. They put a ladder against the building. It is a long ladder—it reaches to the fourth floor. But Johanna is on the fifth floor. The ladder doesn't reach her.

Now the fire is in Johanna's room. Her bed is on fire!

"Help! Help!" she yells again.

"What can we do?" the firefighters ask one another. "We don't have a longer ladder."

"I have an idea," one firefighter says. He gets a short ladder. He climbs up the long ladder with the short ladder in his hand. He stands at the top of the long ladder, turns around, and presses his back against the building. He holds the short ladder above him.

"Come on, Miss, climb down the ladder," he says to Johanna.

"I can't!" Johanna says.

"Yes, you can," the firefighter says. "Just take your time and come down slowly."

Slowly, Johanna climbs down the short ladder. Then she climbs from the short ladder to the long ladder. A few minutes later, she is on the ground.

Johanna is safe, thanks to a smart—and strong—firefighter.

2. VOCABULARY

Match the words and the pictures. Write your answer on the line.

fifth floor   smoke   ladder
climb   ground   get dressed

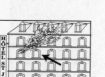

1. ___*fifth floor*___ 2. _____ 3. _____

4. _____ 5. _____ 6. _____

3. COMPREHENSION

UNDERSTANDING THE MAIN IDEAS

Answer the questions. Circle *a* or *b*.

1. Where does Johanna work?
   a. She works in an office in Toronto, Canada.
   (b.) She works at a hotel in Montreal, Canada.

2. Where does Johanna sleep?
   a. She sleeps in her room next to the kitchen.
   b. She sleeps in her room on the fifth floor.

3. Why can't Johanna climb down the long ladder?
   a. The ladder doesn't reach to the fifth floor.
   b. She is afraid to climb down the ladder.

4. How does the firefighter save Johanna?
   a. Johanna jumps from the building, and he catches her.
   b. He holds a short ladder above him, and Johanna climbs down on it.

UNDERSTANDING PRONOUNS

Who is it? What is it? Write the letter of your answer on the line.

1. *It* is in Montreal, Canada. ___b___
2. *She* works at the hotel. _____
3. *They* are yelling, "Fire! Fire!" _____
4. *It* reaches to the fourth floor. _____

a. the people at the hotel

b. the St. James Hotel

c. Johanna O'Connor

d. the long ladder

4. DISCUSSION

Imagine this: Your apartment building is on fire. What do you do?

Read the ideas below. The ideas are in groups of two. One idea is a good idea; the other idea is not a good idea. In a small group, check (✔) the good idea in each group. Then tell the class your group's answers. (The correct answers are on page 82.)

- ☐ **1.** Stay low; the fresh air is near the floor.
- ☐ **2.** Stand up tall; the fresh air is near the ceiling.

- ☐ **3.** Take the elevator down.
- ☐ **4.** Take the stairs down.

- ☐ **5.** When you leave your apartment, close the door and take your keys.
- ☐ **6.** When you leave your apartment, leave the door open so the firefighters can go in.

- ☐ **7.** If you can't leave your apartment, put towels under the door to keep smoke out.
- ☐ **8.** If you can't leave your apartment, leave the door open for the firefighters.

- ☐ **9.** Stay in the bathroom. Get in the shower or bathtub.
- ☐ **10.** Stay near a window.

5. WRITING

Draw a picture and describe it in writing.

1. Listen as your teacher reads the description below:
   I see a tall building. There is one door. The word "HOTEL" is over the door. There are many windows. There is smoke. It is coming out the windows. There is a woman. She is on the fifth floor. She is looking out a window. There is a ladder. It is against the building. It reaches to the fourth floor. There are four firefighters. They are on the street below. There is a short ladder. A firefighter is holding it in his hand.

2. Listen as your teacher reads the description again. On your own paper, draw a picture as your teacher reads.

3. Write five sentences about your picture. Begin your sentences with "There is . . . " or "There are . . . " For example:

   There are many windows.

UNIT 20

1. PRE-READING

Look at the pictures. Listen to your teacher tell the story.

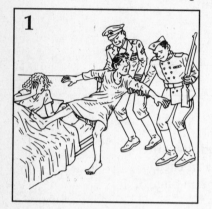

Nothing's Changed

IT is 1944. In a small town in Ukraine, Anton and Anna are asleep in their bed. They are a young married couple. Anton is 21, and Anna is only 15.

Suddenly soldiers come into the bedroom. They pull Anton out of bed. "Come with us!" the soldiers say. It is wartime, and the soldiers want Anton to be a soldier.

One year later, the war ends. After the war, Anton doesn't go back to Ukraine because he doesn't like the government there. He goes to New York City. Anton doesn't write Anna from New York. Anton thinks, "Maybe the police will ask Anna, 'Where is your husband?' If she doesn't know, it is better for her."

Anton is right: The police come to Anna's house and ask her, "Where is your husband?"

"I don't know," Anna says.

"Tell us!" the police say.

"I don't know," Anna says.

For the next nine years, the police come to Anna's house often. "Where is your husband?" they ask Anna. "Tell us!" Finally, Anna marries someone else. The police stop coming to her house.

Anton writes Anna. "I am in New York," he writes. "Come." But it is too late. Anna has a new husband now. She becomes a mother, and later she becomes a grandmother.

In 1994, Anna's husband dies. She writes Anton a letter. "I am free now," she writes. "Do you still have something in your heart for me?"

"Yes, I do," Anton writes back. "I never married again. I loved only you. Come to New York."

Anna arrives at the airport in New York City. She looks for Anton. There he is! After 50 years, there he is! But Anton walks past Anna. Anton remembers his young wife. But he sees only an old woman with gray hair.

"Anton!" Anna says.

"Anna?" Anton asks.

"Yes," Anna answers.

Anton opens his arms wide. "My Anna!" he says.

After 50 years apart, Anton and Anna are together again. "We're very happy," Anton says. "Same like before. Nothing's changed."

2. VOCABULARY

Write the correct word on the line.

apart	asleep	couple
someone else	changed	free

1. Anton is Anna's husband, and Anna is Anton's wife. They are a married

   _____ *couple* _____.

2. Men come into Anton's bedroom late at night. Anton is _____
   in his bed.

3. Anton writes Anna from New York. "Come," he writes. But Anna cannot come

   because she has a new husband. She is married to _____.

4. In 1994, Anna's husband dies, and she can marry Anton. "I am

   _____ now," she writes.

5. Anton says, "Nothing is different. Nothing's _____."

6. From 1944 to 1994, Anton and Anna were not together. They were

   _____.

3. COMPREHENSION

UNDERSTANDING THE MAIN IDEAS

Complete the sentences. Write your answer on the line.

1. Where do Anna and Anton live in 1944?

   They live in _____ *Ukraine* _____.

2. Why do men take Anton from his house?

   They want him to be a _____.

3. Where does Anton go after the war?

   He goes to _____.

4. Why doesn't Anton return to Ukraine?

   He doesn't like the _____.

5. What does Anna answer when the police ask her, "Where is your husband?"

   She answers, "_____."

6. Why does Anton walk past Anna when she is at the airport in New York?

He remembers his young wife, and he sees only _____

_____.

UNDERSTANDING TIME RELATIONSHIPS

When does it happen? Put a check (✔) under 1944, 1945, or 1994.

	1944	1945	1994
1. Anton goes to New York.	☐	☑	☐
2. Soldiers take Anton from his bed.	☐	☐	☐
3. Anna's husband dies.	☐	☐	☐
4. The war ends.	☐	☐	☐
5. Anna goes to New York.	☐	☐	☐
6. It is wartime in Ukraine.	☐	☐	☐

4. DISCUSSION

Anton goes away. Where is he? Anna doesn't know. She waits for nine years. Finally, she marries someone else.

Imagine this: Your husband (or wife) goes away. Where is he (or she)? You don't know. How long do you wait before you marry someone else?

Answer the question. Put your X on the line. Then tell the class your answer.

How long do you wait?

```
├──────────┼──────────────┼──────────────────┼──────────┤
1 year    2 years       5 years          10 years    forever
```

5. WRITING

Read the sentences in the exercise "Understanding Time Relationships." What happens first? What happens second? Copy the sentences in the correct order. For example:

1. It is wartime in Ukraine.

2. Soldiers take Anton from his bed.

Now copy the sentences on your own paper.

To the Student

To prepare for a dictation: Units 1, 7, and 14

1. Look and listen as your teacher says the sentences and acts them out.
2. Act out the sentences with your teacher as your teacher says them.
3. Act out the sentences as your teacher says them. This time, your teacher will not move.
4. Act out the sentences as your teacher says them. This time, repeat the sentences after your teacher.
5. Read the sentences silently.

(You may do steps 1–5 several times.)

Answer Key for Discussion Exercises

UNIT 1

A. There is usually about $600 in the cash register.
B. The man is in prison for about eight years.

UNIT 11

1. On average, people in the United States go to the doctor about 6 times a year.

How many times a year do people in these countries go to the doctor?

Turkey	2
Mexico	2
Sweden	3
Luxembourg	3
Portugal	3
Finland	4
United Kingdom	5
Poland	5
Netherlands	6
Italy	6
Denmark	6
Canada	6
Australia	6
Germany	7
France	7
Austria	7
Belgium	7
Czech Republic	12
Japan	16
Hungary	20

2. People are with the doctor about 26 minutes.
3. The average doctor visit costs $55.
4. The average emergency room visit costs $360.

UNIT 14

This is the judge's decision:

the carpenter	20%	($30,000)
Mr. Williams	40%	($60,000)
Olga	40%	($60,000)

UNIT 15

Toyota and Honda are the two most popular cars with thieves. (Thieves especially like the Toyota Camry, the Honda Accord, and the Honda Civic.) Why do thieves like these cars? They are popular cars, and they last a long time. So, many people need parts for their Toyotas and Hondas. The thieves sell the cars, take them apart, and sell the parts.

UNIT 19

The good ideas are 1, 4, 5, 7, and 10.

To the Teacher

The original newspaper and magazine versions of *All New Easy True Stories* contain information that could not be included in the adaptations. Sometimes the information was too complicated to include; sometimes including it would have made the stories too long for the allotted space. On the other hand, the information—in many cases, the story behind the story—was just too interesting to leave out entirely, so it was decided that additional facts would be given here, in a special "To the Teacher" section.

As you will see from the sophistication of the language, this section is not meant to be read by students. If, however, you think the information adds interest or clarity to a story, you could share it with students. Also included here are specific teaching tips for some of the discussion exercises.

UNIT 1

Give Me the Money!

It is not known if the man who robbed a Circle K convenience store in Texas of 15 dollars was ever arrested.

In the discussion exercise, students are asked to guess how much money, on average, a convenience store has in its cash register. The correct figure is based on the average amount taken when a convenience store is robbed, which is $620. Many convenience stores now have a $50 policy—that is, only $50 is kept in the cash register at one time. All other money is kept in a safe. The other figure—how long a man who uses a gun to rob a convenience store is in prison—is based on the average prison sentence for an armed robbery conviction in the United States, which is 91.4 months.

UNIT 2

License, Please

King Harald was not given a ticket for speeding because Norway's 1814 constitution gives the monarch immunity from prosecution for any crime or misdemeanor. An ordinary citizen would have been fined about 1,000 crowns ($130) for the violation.

Several young politicians in Norway want to change the law. They argue that in a democracy everyone—including the monarch—should be treated equally under the law. The leader of the Socialist Youth Party told the *Aftenposten* newspaper, "It's difficult to defend the fact that it's legal to break the law." Others argue that too much is being made of the incident. Speeding just makes the king seem more human, they say.

Teaching Tip:
The discussion exercise presents an opportunity to discuss bribing police officers, a practice which is accepted in some countries but punishable as a crime in others.

UNIT 3

Mr. Venezuela

The women of Venezuela have a long history of success in beauty pageants. Five Venezuelan women have won the Miss Universe crown, and five have won the Miss World title. When Miss Venezuela doesn't win an international beauty contest, she is almost always among the finalists.

Now the men of Venezuela are getting into the act. The Mr. Venezuela pageant began in 1995 with only fifty contestants. Then, when Mr. Venezuela won the Mr. World title in 1998, the popularity of the contest grew. In 2000, there were 350 contestants.

Contestants are judged in several categories, such as Best Body, Best Smile, Most Photogenic, and, of course, Most Handsome.

UNIT 4

Speed

On the day that Ramya De Silva unexpectedly drove the bus, he had been offered a ride home with a coworker. Concerned that he was imposing, he decided to take the bus. "I am Buddhist," Mr. De Silva says. "I believe in destiny. It was my destiny to be on that bus."

This was not Mr. De Silva's first act of heroism. Just a few months earlier, he had pursued a bank robber and jotted down the license plate number, enabling police to later make an arrest. In his native Sri Lanka, he had driven a delivery truck slowly through a rioting mob to rescue a friend whose home was in the middle of the riot. Mr. De Silva's daughter told the *Los Angeles Times* that her first thought when she learned of her father's heroism was, "Here he goes again."

Mr. De Silva said he regretted very much that he could not save the life of the bus driver, who died of a heart attack.

UNIT 5

Grandfather Hada's Favorite Soup

Mochi, a seasonal delicacy in Japan, is made from very glutinous rice. It is difficult to chew and swallow, and it is not uncommon for elderly people to choke on it. During one holiday season from December 26 to January 3, six elderly people in Tokyo died after choking on mochi, and six others were hospitalized in critical condition. The Tokyo Fire Department issued a warning that seniors should cut mochi in small pieces and eat it only in the presence of others.

Grandfather Hada's daughter had worked as a nurse's aide, caring for the elderly. At that time, she had been told by a nurse that a vacuum cleaner could be used to extract mochi from someone's throat. She remembered the tip when her own father choked on mochi.

Teaching Tip:
This story invites a discussion about foods that are choking hazards to small children. You might want to write on the board a list of foods that children like to eat. For example:

hot dogs   grapes
rice   bananas
hard candy   pizza

Ask students (perhaps working in small groups) to guess which foods children in the United States and Canada most often choke on. (The correct answers are: hot dogs, hard candy, and grapes.)

UNIT 6

Handsome Again?

Santino Deng belongs to a Sudanese tribe called the Dinka. He described the extraction of his six bottom teeth to the *Wall Street Journal:* "His father held his head, and for ten minutes a tribesman twisted the tip of a spear between his teeth until they fell out. 'It hurt very much,' he recalls, 'but none of us cried.'"

Although Mr. Deng says people in his village who still have front bottom teeth are taunted as "dogs," he doesn't care; he desperately wants his teeth back. A professor at the dental school at the University of Nebraska is attaching titanium implants under Deng's gumline. Later, the implants will be capped with artificial teeth. The process takes months. Two dental-supply companies are paying for the procedure, which five men from Sudan, including Mr. Deng, are undergoing.

There is a large Sudanese settlement in Nebraska, and most of these Sudanese have come to regard the ritual tooth extraction as a misguided practice. Still, they hold no ill will toward the elders who pulled their teeth. They say the tribal elders "thought they were doing us a favor."

Anthropologists do not know the origin of the practice, although they speculate it may have begun during an outbreak of tetanus, or "lockjaw." Perhaps the teeth were originally removed so that children suffering from the disease could eat.

UNIT 7

A Super Soaker and a Super Kid

The super kid is actually named Isiah, not Daniel, but the name was changed to make it easier for teachers and students to pronounce.

Isiah was honored in a ceremony at the Watsonville, CA, police department for his quick thinking. The puppies, both Labradors, recovered from the heat and have been adopted.

Teaching Tip:
This story invites a conversation about the dangers of hot weather, especially to those who work outdoors. You might wish to introduce the conversation by asking your students to imagine this: You are working outside in hot weather. You know that hot weather can be dangerous. Stop working immediately if you . . .

1. feel dizzy.
2. have a headache.
3. have a stomachache.
4. are breathing fast.
5. are breathing slowly.
6. have a high temperature.
7. have a fast heartbeat.
8. have a slow heartbeat.
9. can't think clearly.

Students check seven answers and compare their answers with a partner's. (The correct answers are 1, 2, 3, 4, 6, 7, and 9.)

UNIT 8

The Flying Lesson

Barbara Yeninas, age 56, and her flight instructor, age 65, were practicing landings at a municipal airport in Florida when another plane essentially landed on top of them. The 19-year-old pilot of the larger plane had not seen the smaller plane because of the design of his plane: It has a low-wing design, and the pilot cannot see the area blocked by the wings. He said that he knew he had hit something, but he couldn't see what it was. "I knew I'd landed," he said. "But I couldn't figure out why I was sitting so high off the ground."

Barbara's instructor said Barbara "handled it very, very well. Her biggest worry was how to break the news to her husband, who I guess wasn't very enthusiastic about her taking up flying lessons in the first place."

UNIT 9

Hawaiian Vacation

To simplify the story, the boy is described as a non-swimmer. Actually, the boy does swim but got into trouble during an underwater breath-holding contest with his brother. The two boys were trying to stay underwater for one minute and 45 seconds. The boy remembers passing the one-minute-and-40-second mark, and then he blacked out. When he was pulled from the water, he had no pulse and no heartbeat.

Twenty-one-year old Quentin is a corporal in the U.S. Marines. He was returning to the United States from a tour of duty and was on liberty in Hawaii when he saved the boy's life. His commanding officer said, "We recently had CPR classes, and he was one of the few who were actually taking notes, so this was fresh in his mind. I'm very proud of him." Quentin Gwynn was awarded a commendation from the governor of Hawaii for his "courageous actions."

The "high rock" from which Quentin jumped was sixty feet above the water.

Teaching Tip:
In the discussion/writing exercise, students write four sentences about a vacation spot. If your students have little experience writing independently, you might want to make the writing a collaborative effort. You could, for example, simply ask students to describe popular vacations spots orally while you write their sentences on the board.

UNIT 10

Election Day

In the story, Herb (Casey is a pseudonym) ran for mayor of his town. Actually, that was not the office he desired. He was running to become the Democratic candidate for the Governor's Council of Massachusetts. In the *All New Easy True Stories* version of the story, the office was changed to "mayor" to make the vocabulary suitable for beginning learners.

The eight-member Governor's Council approves criminal pardons and confirms judges nominated by the governor. Mr. Casey had served on the council for almost twenty years and was running for reelection. He received 14,715 votes; his opponent received 14,716. If he had voted—and voted for himself—the election would have resulted in a tie. The tie would have been broken by town Democratic committees in Casey's district.

UNIT 11

The Best Doctor

Fifty-seven-year old Connie Munro injured her knee dancing. She had surgery on her knee in the spring, but in the fall she was still limping. Then she encountered the bear. When she spotted it, the bear was only 15 feet away. She ran around her car once and then, with the bear in pursuit, sprinted toward a building. "I'm not kidding, I thought I was permanently disabled," she said. "The bear has given me a present. I can walk normally."

It is not unusual for bears to come into Juneau, where Ms. Munro lives, in the spring and fall. The animal scurried off before police could catch it.

UNIT 12

The Bottle

Ake Viking wrote his note in 1955, and Sebastiano Puzzo, a Sicilian fisherman, found it in May 1957. So, it took the bottle two years to make its way from Sweden to Sicily.

Mr. Puzzo did not read English, so he brought the note home for his 18-year-old daughter to translate. She and Ake married in the autumn of 1958.

Teaching Tip:
In the discussion exercise, students put their X on a YES/NO continuum in response to the question, "Will Ake and Paolina be happy together?" The continuum could also be put on the blackboard; students stand at the place that reflects their opinion.

UNIT 13

Hold On, Joe

Joe Thompson remembers bouncing off at least three wires before his foot caught on one. It took 20 minutes to rescue him because the power lines above him had to be turned off before the rescue ladder could be raised.

Joe's father got a call first from the police and then from Joe. "The police told me Joe was hanging on for dear life," he said. "I didn't know they meant he literally was hanging on for dear life." He told a reporter from the Associated Press, "Don't forget: This is a great story to remind people to wear seat belts."

UNIT 14

Whose Money Is It?

Louise Stamberg, an immigrant to the U.S. from Yugoslavia, bought her house in the early 1900s and lived there until she died in 1958. During the Depression, Ms. Stamberg lost confidence in banks and began storing her savings in coffee cans that she placed above the kitchen ceiling. The statement in the story, "This money is for Olga," is intentionally ambiguous. It is not known if Ms. Stamberg intended that all the money would go to Olga or that only the money in the cans marked "Olga" would go to her.

The carpenter who found the money did not tell anyone about his discovery and began quietly spending the money. Because the bills were old, they had different colors and markings from modern cash. Workers at the supermarket where the carpenter was spending money thought it was counterfeit and called the police, who called the Secret Service. The Secret Service determined that the money was legal, but that spending it was perhaps not. The carpenter was forced to turn over the remainder of the $150,000 (he had already spent $30,000) until a judge could decide who was the rightful owner. The judge ruled that the carpenter could keep the $30,000 he had already spent. The remaining money was divided between Olga and Brian Williams.

UNIT 15

The Silver Porsche

The 26-year-old owner of the Porsche told the *Yomiuri Shimbun* newspaper that he was initially dismayed when his first Internet search yielded 100,000 hits. But when he began narrowing the search, the number of hits rapidly declined until finally there was only one Porsche with the same mileage as his.

The Porsche was a Boxster, which sells for approximately $50,000. Tokyo police believe that organized crime might have been behind the theft.

UNIT 16

An Easy Job

After Anne fell into the glue, she went outside and tried to hose it off, but was worried about the glue drying on the floor. So, she decided to lay down the vinyl—which took only 20 minutes—and then clean the glue off herself. She told a Maryland newspaper, the *Capitol Gazette,* that she doubted she would tackle any more home improvement projects herself but is happy with the way the floor turned out. She said she saved $700 by laying the vinyl herself and added, "The bottom line is the floor looks good."

UNIT 17

The Pet Rabbit

Maureen Nunn is host of a nationally syndicated cable TV series, *Everyday Heroes,* on how ordinary people can change the world. A former ESL teacher, she was enthusiastic about having this story included in *All New Easy True Stories.* Mrs. Nunn says the story, which first appeared in Kay Allenbaugh's *Chocolate for a Mother's Heart* under the title "The Rare Mongolian Rabbit," is "100% true."

Mr. Nunn's job had been "phased out," and Mrs. Nunn, with three children under the age of five and a fourth due in three months, was not able to support the family by returning to teaching. By the time she encountered Jeff at the supermarket, her husband had been out of work for months, and their food budget was nonexistent. "What," Mrs. Nunn wondered, "is the proper etiquette for begging for food for one's children?" She blurted out, "We have a rare Mongolian rabbit! I'd be interested in purchasing food for the rabbit." Jeff replied, "Since it's just a rabbit, there won't be any charge."

During the following months, Jeff packed the "rabbit food" boxes with peanut butter, soup, cheese, laundry detergent, milk, juice, and butter. All were outdated or damaged items that were otherwise still good but would have been thrown away.

UNIT 18

The Birthday Present

The $1,000 coat that Joe bought for his wife was made of cashmere. When he set the coat down so that he could shovel snow for his sister-in-law, he placed it near some garbage that was put out for the trash collector.

A sanitation supervisor in Madison, Wisconsin, where Joe lives, said, "This happens quite often but not often does it turn out good." He added, "We were kind of chuckling in the office about it. We were thinking that the guy probably bought his wife a blender and wanted to cover it up saying he bought her an expensive coat."

UNIT 19

The Fire

The rescue of Johanna O'Connor by firefighter John Beckingham is described in the 1881 book *Fighting the Flames* by William McRobie. It is one of several rescues recounted by McRobie, who was a captain in the Montreal Fire Brigade. He stated that he wrote the book "so that the citizens of Montreal will understand something of the feelings of heroism and daring which animate the members of the brigade."

McRobie commended the courage of both the firefighter and Johanna O'Connor, calling her rescue with two ladders "a feat I believe unparalleled in history, for while it may not appear much in my simple manner of describing it, let some of my female readers that have never descended a ladder before try to come out of a first-story window onto a ladder. I feel safe in saying that nine out of ten will back out and not risk it. When we take into consideration the fact that Miss O'Connor was eighty feet from the ground, and the top ladder very unsteady, she must have been a girl of remarkably strong nerves and undoubted courage. I repeat, I do not believe the feat has ever been equaled."

UNIT 20

Nothing's Changed

Anton was pulled out of bed by German soldiers who wanted him to work on a state farm in Germany.

Anton did not contact Anna from New York because he had a reputation as an ardent anti-Communist. He feared that any contact with her might endanger her safety under the Soviet government. For nine years Anna did not hear a word from Anton. Not knowing if Anton was dead or alive, and tired of being regularly threat-

ened and questioned by the KGB, she finally remarried.

Anton says he understands why Anna remarried. "I don't blame her," he told the Associated Press. "So many years and big pressures on her. Maybe I blame her if the KGB don't bother her, don't beat her, but not now." Translating for Anna, who speaks little English, Anton said, "She told me she was always thinking about me, even when she was married." Then he added his own thought. "That's first love."

For a reporter from the *Hartford Courant*, Anton described the scene at the airport. "She had a babushka on. I look. I see this woman. After she sits, I walk away, I turn back. I look again. She sees me. Then we jump. I always thought that maybe some day it would happen."

Teaching Tip:
In the discussion exercise, students put their X on a continuum in response to the question, "How long do you wait?" The continuum could also be put on the blackboard; students stand at the place that reflects their answer.

ABOUT THE AUTHOR

Sandra Heyer has taught English to adults, young adults, university students, and middle- and high-school students. She currently teaches adult learners in Whitewater, Wisconsin, in a community-based program she co-founded and coordinates.

The True Stories reading series evolved from materials she prepared for her students in an effort to provide them with readings that were both high-interest and comprehensible. She continues to develop and pilot new material for the series in her own classroom.

ACKNOWLEDGMENTS

I wish to thank...

- Callie Gwynn, who sent photos of her son Quentin, along with newspaper accounts of the rescue;
- Henrick Martinell at the Consulate General of Sweden, who provided information about the uniform of a Swedish sailor;
- Gil Miranda, who sent the story of Louise Stamberg's stashed money from the *Plain Dealer*;
- Reference librarian Josée Kourie at the Bibliothèque de Montréal, who verified the story of the rescue with two ladders;
- Student artists Marivel Jaime and Gabriela Marquez, who provided the drawings for units 5 and 8;
- My congenial colleagues Jorge Islas and Anjie Martin, Whitewater (Wisconsin) Community Education, who graciously accommodated field testing;
- Robert Ruvo, who skillfully guided this book through its final stages; and
- John Barnes and Laura LeDrean at Longman, who gave me just the right amount of direction and help.

TEXT CREDITS

<u>Give Me the Money!</u>
The two figures in the discussion exercise are from the following sources: 1) The figure $620 is from a Federal Bureau of Investigations (FBI) 2000 report. 2) The average prison sentence for someone convicted of armed robbery, 91.4 months, is from a U.S. Department of Justice 2000 report.

<u>Grandfather Hada's Favorite Soup</u>
The idea for the discussion exercise is from *Zero Prep* by Laurel Pollard and Natalie Hess, Alta Book Center Publishers, 1997. ("What I Like to Eat," p. 5)

<u>A Super Soaker and a Super Kid</u>
The eight symptoms of heat stroke listed in the To the Teacher section are from the Web site Web.MD.com.

<u>The Best Doctor</u>
The figures for the discussion exercise are from the following sources: 1) average number of annual visits to the doctor: Organization for Economic Co-Operation and Development; 2) average time spent with patients: the research of Dr. Harold Luft, University of California at San Francisco; 3) average doctor visit cost and average E.R. visit cost: the Web site of the American Institute for Preventive Medicine.

<u>The Birthday Present</u>
The idea for the discussion/writing exercise is from *Zero Prep* by Laurel Pollard and Natalie Hess, Alta Book Center Publishers, 1997. ("Gift Exchange," p. 75)

<u>The Fire</u>
The "good ideas" in the discussion exercise are from the Web site of the Honolulu Fire Department.

The pre-dictation activity in Units 1, 7, and 14 is inspired by James Asher's Total Physical Response Method. These particular steps are recommended by Laurel Pollard and Natalie Hess in *Zero Prep,* Alta Book Center Publishers, 1997. ("Act It Out," p. 85)

The discussion activity in Units 8 and 17 is suggested by Sharron Bassano and Mary Ann Christison in *Drawing Out,* Alta Book Center Publishers.

PHOTO CREDITS

UNIT 1
Give Me the Money!
© Susan Van Etten/Photo Edit

UNIT 2
License, Please
Scanpix Scandinavia

UNIT 3
Mr. Venezuela
AP/ Wide World Photos

UNIT 4
Speed
Los Angeles Times photo by Al Schaben

UNIT 5
Grandfather Hada's Favorite Soup
Satsuko Yoshizuka

UNIT 6
Handsome Again?
Wall Street Journal

UNIT 7
A Super Soaker and a Super Kid
Courtesy of Tarmo Hannula / Register Pajaronian

UNIT 8
The Flying Lesson
David Mitchell

UNIT 9
Hawaiian Vacation
Honolulu Advertiser

UNIT 10
Jack Star/PhotoLink/Getty Images

UNIT 11
The Best Doctor
Galen Rowell / Corbis

UNIT 12
The Bottle
Getty Images

UNIT 13
Hold On, Joe
Fred Farmer/AP/Wide World Photos

UNIT 14
Whose Money Is It?
Ralph J. Meyers ©1988 The Plain Dealer (This is not the house in the story.)

UNIT 15
The Silver Porsche
Courtesy of Edmunds.com

UNIT 16
An Easy Job
Paul Quigley

UNIT 17
The Pet Rabbit
Getty Images

UNIT 18
The Birthday Present
© Comstock IMAGES

UNIT 19
The Fire
adapted by Don Martinetti from L'Opinion publique, 27 March 1873, provided courtesy of musée d'archéologie et d'histoire de Montréal

UNIT 20
Nothing's Changed
Tony Bacewicz / Hartford Courant

Answer Key

UNIT 1

Vocabulary
2. cashier   3. $20 bill   4. counter   5. gun   6. bag

Remembering Details
2. a   3. b   4. b   5. a

Reviewing the Story
2. opens   3. shows   4. money   5. all   6. store

UNIT 2

Vocabulary
2. follow   3. curve   4. pull over   5. license   6. king

Remembering Details
2. Norway   3. fast   4. ten kilometers over the speed limit   5. king
of Norway

Making Connections
2. e   3. c   4. a   5. b

UNIT 3

Vocabulary
2. Venezuela   3. winner   4. lift weights   5. model

Remembering Details
2. intelligent / beautiful   3. children / men   4. doctor / model
5. pizza / chicken   6. meat / candy

Making Connections
2. c   3. a   4. d

UNIT 4

Vocabulary
2. behind   3. steering wheel   4. brake   5. passengers   6. hero

Remembering Details
2. b   3. b   4. b   5. b   6. a

Understanding Pronouns
2. e   3. a   4. b   5. f   6. d

UNIT 5

Vocabulary
2. throat   3. stuck   4. breathe   5. check

Remembering Details
2. cake / soup   3. fish / chicken   4. potato / rice   5. make / eat   6.
teeth / throat   7. white / purple   8. vegetables / mochi

Making Connections
2. d   3. a   4. b   5. c

UNIT 6

Vocabulary
2. village   3. handsome   4. painful   5. soft   6. expensive

Understanding the Main Ideas
2. a   3. b   4. b

Reviewing the Story
2. custom   3. handsome   4. eat   5. dentist   6. again

UNIT 7

Vocabulary
2. puppies   3. worried   4. locked   5. fills   6. cool

Remembering Details
2. hot summer day   3. two puppies are in the car   4. thirsty
5. one hour   6. police officer breaks a car window

Understanding Pronouns
2. e   3. c   4. a   5. b

UNIT 8

Vocabulary
2. lessons   3. landing   4. practicing   5. noise   6. on top of

Remembering Details
2. small airplane   3. on top of the small airplane   4. Sorry. I was
landing, too. I didn't see you.   5. two airplanes

Who Says It?
2. b   3. a   4. c

UNIT 9

Vocabulary
2. CPR   3. gone   4. credit card   5. free   6. meals

Understanding the Main Ideas
2. b   3. a   4. a   5. b

Understanding Sequence
2. 1, 2   3. 2,1   4. 1,2   5. 1, 2

UNIT 10

Vocabulary
2. knock on doors   3. mail letters   4. give speeches   5. vote
6. call people on the phone

Understanding the Main Ideas
1. b   2. c   3. b

Remembering Details
He puts up signs. He calls people on the phone. He mails letters.
He knocks on doors and talks to people.

UNIT 11

Vocabulary
2. hurts   3. limp   4. surgery   5. toward   6. dangerous

Making Connections
2. f   3. c   4. b   5. d   6. a

Reviewing the Story
2. still   3. work   4. bear   5. building   6. knee

UNIT 12

Vocabulary
2. ship   3. address   4. bottle   5. throw   6. sea

Remembering Details
2. nothing to do   3. 18 years old   4. one year   5. English

Making Connections
2. c   3. a   4. b

UNIT 13

Vocabulary
2. hit   3. roll over   4. grab   5. hang   6. hold on

Making Connections
2. e   3. a   4. d   5. b

Understanding Sequence
2. 1,2   3. 2,1   4. 2,1

UNIT 14

Vocabulary
2. ceiling   3. remodel   4. hires   5. found   6. judge

Understanding the Main Ideas
2. a   3. a   4. b   5. a

Who Says It?
2. b   3. c   4. a

UNIT 15

Vocabulary
2. used-car dealer   3. click on   4. hits   5. type   6. scratch

Remembering Details
2. German car   3. silver   4. 15,000 kilometers   5. sold it

Reviewing the Story
2. back   3. gets on   4. Shop   5. Used   6. kilometers   7. sure
8. police   9. later

UNIT 16

Vocabulary
2. spreads   3. quickly   4. take off   5. Thanks anyway   6. hang up

Understanding the Main Ideas
2. a   3. a   4. b

Finding More Information
2. e   3. c   4. a   5. b

UNIT 17

Vocabulary
2. pet   3. anymore   4. it doesn't matter   5. manager   6. quietly

Understanding the Main Ideas
2. b   3. b   4. a   5. b

Understanding Dialog
2. a   3. d   4. b

UNIT 18

Vocabulary
2. sister-in-law   3. shoveling snow   4. gone   5. dump   6. empty

Understanding the Main Ideas
2. a   3. b   4. b   5. a

Remembering Details
old onions, old shoes, empty cans, old potatoes, old clothes, the coat

UNIT 19

Vocabulary
2. smoke   3. get dressed   4. ladder   5. climb   6. ground

Understanding the Main Ideas
2. b   3. a   4. b

Understanding Pronouns
2. c   3. a   4. e   5. d

UNIT 20

Vocabulary
2. asleep   3. someone else   4. free   5. changed   6. apart

Understanding the Main Ideas
2. soldier   3. New York City   4. government   5. I don't know
6. an old woman with gray hair

Understanding Time Relationships
2. 1944   3. 1994   4. 1945   5. 1994   6. 1944